PREDICTING
YOUR FUTURE

PREDICTING YOUR FUTURE

THE COMPLETE BOOK OF
DIVINATION

 JANE STRUTHERS

C&B

COLLINS & BROWN

To Chelsey,

WITH LOVE AND THANKS FOR EVERYTHING

First published in Great Britain in 1997
by Collins & Brown Limited
London House
Great Eastern Wharf
Parkgate Road
London SW11 4NQ

1 3 5 7 9 8 6 4 2

British Library Cataloguing-in-Publication Data: A catalogue record for this
book is available from the British Library.

ISBN 1 85585 427 9 (hardback edition)
ISBN I 85585 476 7 (paperback edition)

Conceived, edited and designed by Collins & Brown Limited

Editor: Alison Wormleighton
Designer: Roger Daniels
Artwork: Jacqueline Mair

Reproduction by Daylight Colour Art
Printed and bound in Hong Kong by South Seas International

CONTENTS

Introduction

Ever since we began to think, we have used a huge variety of methods to determine what the future holds for us. Many of these techniques have been passed down through the generations, and they've come from all corners of the globe.

The positions of the stars, the appearance of comets in the sky, the fall of the dice, the patterns created by an animal's entrails, the visions in a crystal ball and many other techniques all belong under the general heading of the mantic, or prophetic, arts. They enjoyed a tremendous vogue during the nineteenth century, which was a time when interest in psychic matters blossomed. Maybe this was a rebellion against the newly industrialized age, in which machines were taking over from man. And perhaps that's why these arts are experiencing another revival now, in the age of the computer chip and the great god science.

Sceptics may refer to the mantic arts as fortune-telling (a phrase that is frequently used pejoratively); yet these techniques can tell you a lot more than simply what's going to happen next week or next month. They can give you an invaluable insight into your own personality, crystallizing your ideas and helping you to reach decisions that have been difficult until now. They can also access your intuition and help to develop your latent psychic powers.

The mantic arts cover a remarkable range of techniques, from the simple to the extremely complicated. Seven of the most popular methods are described in this book – the tarot, cartomancy (reading playing cards), Sun sign astrology, Chinese astrology, palmistry, numerology and dowsing with pendulums.

With the possible exception of the tarot, these techniques use items that you will already own. Indeed, you may already own a pack of tarot cards. Cartomancy simply requires an ordinary deck of playing cards. For dowsing, if you don't already have a pendulum, you can make your own by suspending a ring from a piece of string. Sun sign and Chinese astrology only require someone's date of birth for you to gain an intriguingly accurate insight into their character and the relationship that they have with you. Palmistry can be practised anywhere – once you've learned the rudiments, not only can you read the hands of friends and family, but you can also study from afar the hands of complete strangers while sitting on the bus, holding a conversation, even watching television. Numerology simply requires someone's date of birth or name. From these elementary pieces of information you can construct a complex picture of their personality, including the hidden emotional side that they don't let anyone see. Pendulums have a dual purpose – they can supply the answers to questions

Facing page: An astrological illustration from an English psalter of c.1170. Above: Some of the constellations in the ceiling from the Sala del mappamondo *fresco by G. De Vecchi and da Reggio*

about your future, and they can also help you to dowse for lost objects, water, and anything else you're looking for. Together, these techniques will provide a wide range of predictive skills that you can draw on whenever necessary.

As you experiment, you may find that one technique works far better for you than all the rest. Perhaps you have a particular affinity for it, or it simply produces more accurate results than anything else. Alternatively, you may find that all the techniques work for you in their different ways, so you can pick and choose according to what you want to know.

The techniques in this book offer a means of developing your own intuition. What you must remember, even if you have staggeringly accurate results, is that you're the one who's doing the work, not your tarot cards, your pendulum or whatever else you're using. It's your interpretation of these results that's important, not the

results themselves. Avoid confusing the medium with the message. For instance, it's a common fallacy that tarot cards are invested with special powers, but they aren't. They are simply inanimate objects that you've chosen for the purposes of divination. You're the one with the special powers. Eventually, if you are very gifted and intuitive, you'll find that you don't really need the tarot cards, the numerology or whichever technique you're using, because you already know the answers to the questions you want to ask.

You may also find that your experience of what each of these techniques means is different from what's described in this book, or any other book, come to that. Don't imagine that you've got it wrong – instead, you are getting it right because you're discovering what these techniques mean to you, and how they apply in your life. That's when your interpretations will really start to take flight. Enjoy the ride!

The Tarot

Of all the predictive techniques described in this book, none carries quite the

emotional baggage and powerful significance of the tarot. To some people, this is

the devil's picture-book, a collection of cards that will bring about doom and destruction.

To others, it's a predictive tool that is capable of pinpointing events and emotions with

astonishing accuracy and subtlety. And some people believe that its greatest

benefits lie in its ability to highlight the psychology behind events, to reveal

someone's motives and to enable them to understand themselves better.

THE ORIGINS of the tarot have long since been forgotten, although there are plenty of theories to choose from. Some authorities claim that the tarot originated in Ancient Egypt (hence the symbolism found on many of the cards), while others believe it came from China, India or Italy. Whoever is correct, the tarot had certainly arrived in Italy by the early fifteenth century, because a particularly beautiful pack was probably painted by Antonio Cicognara for the important Colleoni family of Bergamo. From there, the cards gradually became better known and in the late fifteenth century the Marseilles tarot pack, created by B P Grimaud, became popular because the images it portrayed had moved away from the fine-art allegorical tradition of Italian packs and concentrated on ease of interpretation. The Marseilles tarot is still used today.

In due course, the tarot was taken up by other occultists who ascribed various meanings to it. One of the most popular versions, which has inspired many other packs, is the Rider-Waite deck. This was developed in 1910 by A E Waite, a member of the Hermetic Order of the Golden Dawn, an esoteric society founded in London in 1881. Among his fellow members were the poet W B Yeats, Mrs Oscar Wilde and Aleister Crowley, the magician who was later dubbed 'the wickedest man in the world'. They believed that the tarot was the key to all other esoteric subjects, including astrology.

Today, a rich variety of tarot packs is available. As well as the standard rectangular shape, you can buy circular cards (beautiful, but difficult to shuffle) or huge rectangles (not for people with small hands), as well as packs from all corners of the globe, including Europe, Japan, Russia and Kashmir. Some decks bear images that are instantly recognizable to people familiar with the

A fourteenth-century tarot reading

classic tarot pack, while others are so different as to be almost a new form of divination.

DISCOVERING THE TAROT

A classic tarot pack consists of 78 cards – the 22 cards of the Major Arcana and the 56 cards of the Minor Arcana. The Major Arcana is a set of trump cards decorated with pictures which symbolize man's journey through life, showing all the setbacks and opportunities that he meets along the way. The first card, the Fool, is not numbered, so the World, which is the final card of the Major Arcana, bears the number 21. The 56 cards of the Minor Arcana are very similar to an ordinary pack of playing cards. In fact, it is believed that ordinary playing cards were developed from the Minor Arcana. The main distinctions between the two are that each tarot suit has four court cards (King, Queen, Knight and Page) instead of the three of ordinary playing cards, and the suits have different names. In the tarot, these are Cups or Vessels (which correspond to Hearts in playing cards); Wands, Staves or Staffs (Clubs); Pentacles or Coins (Diamonds); and Swords (Spades).

CHOOSING A TAROT PACK

If you've never used the tarot before, or are doubtful of your abilities to memorize the meanings of all 78 cards at once, it is best to buy a pack with illustrations on the pip (numbered) cards of the Minor Arcana. These will help you to remember their basic meanings and will provide plenty of clues for more subtle interpretations. If possible, choose the pack yourself, rather than having one bought for you (although tradition dictates it should be the other way round), because finding a set of tarot cards that you like is a very personal business. What suits one person will not suit another, so visit a shop that sells a wide variety of packs and spend time browsing through them. Choose a set of cards that fits your hands – no matter how beautiful they may be, it's extremely frustrating if you can't shuffle the cards properly because they're too large and keep falling out of your hands. Very big cards require a vast amount of table space when you lay them out – this can be a disadvantage, especially when using large, complicated spreads.

The designs of some tarot packs have few connections with traditional tarot meanings and more to do with esoteric or cultural beliefs. These may greatly appeal to you, or you may find them confusing. It doesn't matter which design you use – it can be a copy of the classic eighteenth-century Marseilles pack or a contemporary design based on Arthurian legends – provided it's one you like and with which you have an instinctive empathy. If you don't like your tarot cards you won't use them, so choose a pack that you truly enjoy and that triggers your imagination and intuition. It may take a while before you find the perfect pack, but the search can be very enjoyable. You may even end up with several packs, all of which you use at one time or another.

GETTING USED TO THE TAROT

When you first unwrap your new tarot pack, enjoy looking at the cards. Spend some time studying each one in turn, and see if any instinctive impressions come to you. At this stage it's a good idea to look at each card and then read the description of its meaning. Study the card carefully for any pictorial clues that will imprint its meaning in your mind. For instance, when you look at the Sun, which symbolizes creativity and happiness, you could imagine the relaxed, contented feeling that one gets when basking in the warmth of the Sun's rays. If you're astrologically minded, you could remember that Leo is ruled by the Sun, and is the sign of creativity.

The next step is to shuffle the cards well. Like ordinary playing cards, they won't work properly if they remain in numerical order. A good way to mix them up well is to spread them out over a flat surface and swish them around with your hands, then collect them together, turning round any that are upside down or back to front. You can now give them a good shuffle, then cut them several times if you wish.

Opinion is divided on how you should look after your cards. Some people don't give them any special treatment, simply storing them in their original box after use. Others like to treat their tarot cards with special consideration or in a rit-ualistic manner. This is usually because they believe that the tarot must be protected from out-side vibrations, and that a new tarot pack needs to be charged with the owner's energy. If you like this idea, you can influence a new pack of cards with your vibrations either by placing them under your pillow before you go to sleep, or simply by looking at them and holding them.

Whenever you put the cards away, you can wrap them in a piece of black or purple silk, which is believed to protect them from outside psychic forces, and then place them in a wooden box. Even if you don't believe in such things as psychic protection, you may still enjoy the ritual involved, which gives the cards added impor-tance. When you give readings, you may want to spread out your cards on a specially chosen piece of fabric which throws the cards into relief and makes their illustrations more vivid.

Whether you store your cards in a special box or in a plastic bag, you should not let other people handle them except when you're giving them readings, just as you should never handle anyone else's cards without their permission. Otherwise, the cards will pick up unwanted vibrations.

The Moon, from the Cicognara tarot pack

GIVING A READING

If you've never used the tarot before, wait until you're relatively familiar with the cards before giving any serious readings. Otherwise, both you and the person for whom you're reading the cards are likely to become fed up with the long pauses while you frantically look up a card's meaning or vainly try to remember it. So, at first, read the cards for yourself but try to resist the temptation to look up the meanings immediately. Instead, study the illustrations on the cards and see what comes to you. Only when you have searched your memory should you actually read the interpreta-tion of the card.

When trying to remember the meaning of a Minor Arcana card you can give yourself clues by analysing the significance of the suit and the number. (Brief descriptions of each number are given in this chapter; more detailed ones appear in the numerology chapter.) Let's imagine that you're staring at the Four of Pentacles and trying desperately to remember what it means. First, think of what Pentacles represents – money, material possessions, the way you organize work and business. Then think of what four means – completion, stability, structure. You can then put these two meanings together and, perhaps helped by the illustration on the card, deduce that the Four of Pentacles symbolizes a healthy financial situation, about which the person probably feels quite satisfied, but there's a danger that this could lead to complacency and a materialistic, possibly even greedy, outlook.

As with all the other techniques described in this book, it is very important not to frighten anyone when you give them a reading. Some people are especially wary of the tarot, believing that it is somehow allied to black magic (probably partly thanks to its associations with the self-styled 'Beast', Aleister Crowley) or is so accurate that its predictions are set in stone. Neither of these claims is true. When you deal out the cards for a spread, they are a snapshot of the potential of that moment. If you ask the same question and deal out the cards the following day, you'll probably get a slightly different answer. Some of the cards might be the same while others will have changed, because even in that short time your circumstances – or your attitude towards them – will have altered. So although the tarot can be extremely accurate, it isn't infallible and what it predicts does not automatically happen. Above all, remember that we have free will and can alter our destinies.

One of the main messages of the tarot concerns change, and many cards deal with this theme. Some cards are wonderfully positive and happy, others urge caution, while a few seem extremely negative at first, yet they always have an underlying meaning that's much more positive. However, it has to be said that some cards – the Hanged Man, Death, the Tower and the Ten of Swords – often bear images that can be alarming. Always reassure your questioner that choosing

the Death card or the Hanged Man doesn't mean they are about to die or to be strung up. Instead, they are facing major changes in their life.

When giving someone a tarot reading, always err on the side of caution. If you deal out what can only be described as a very negative spread, full of Swords (which represent problems and, sometimes, arguments) and some of the more difficult Major Arcana cards, you can issue a few carefully worded warnings but avoid putting the fear of God into the other person. Remember that we can choose either to act on the suggestions that the cards give us or to completely ignore them. Sometimes the cards appear to play games with you, or give you nonsensical messages, in which case it's best to leave them alone for a day.

In other words, what appears in a reading is not an inevitable outcome. Of course, if you're giving a reading for someone who you know has money worries, and these are emphasized in the reading, with perhaps a card of massive change (such as the Tower) as the outcome, then there may be rough times ahead, but this doesn't always follow. The person having the reading may take avoiding action, so the prophecy of the Tower is never fulfilled.

In general, though, you shouldn't place too much emphasis on the really negative cards unless they are dogging someone's footsteps by appearing in most of their readings. Even then, the events that these cards foretell may never happen for all sorts of reasons. Nevertheless, as you become more adept at the tarot you will discover just how accurate it can be, pinpointing emotions and events with relentless (and sometimes agonizing) precision.

Choose your words carefully when discussing sensitive emotional topics, too. For instance, if the questioner is worried about a close relationship and all the cards suggest that they are being manipulated or deceived, you must be careful how you say this. If necessary, play it down – you don't want to send them home in tears. If you suspect that they're being swindled, you can drop hints by suggesting that they should thoroughly scrutinize their finances, but you should never say, 'Don't you realize that your lover/daughter/accountant is bleeding you dry?' Be equally circumspect when dealing with health matters – don't make dire forecasts.

If you read your own cards, you might find it interesting to keep notes of each reading. Don't forget to write down the date and time, because you can then refer to your interpretations at a later date to see if the predictions have come true, if you interpreted the cards correctly and if the cards provided clues as to the timing of these events. There will inevitably be a few disappointments (what happened to that promised lottery win?) but there will also be some triumphs.

REVERSED CARDS

A reversed card is one that appears upside down in a reading. Tarot readers disagree about whether this is significant. Some assign a separate meaning to a reversed card, while others prefer to ignore it and simply turn it round the right way. Only upright meanings are given in this chapter because they present quite enough of a challenge for you without having to learn 78 reversed meanings as well. However, if you wish, you can take note of any reversed cards, applying the theory that their reversal means the outcome of the card will be delayed for a while. As you become more experienced in reading tarot cards, you'll discover whether this theory works for you. Each tarot reader has slightly different interpretations of each card, so let your intuition tell you what the reversed cards mean in a reading.

BEGINNING A READING

When you give someone a reading, it is best done at a table in relaxed surroundings. It is also best done in private – you don't want to be surrounded by inquisitive onlookers or spectators who think it's all a huge joke. If one of you is uncomfortable, you'll find it hard to relax and this could affect the success of the reading.

Sit opposite your questioner (the person for whom you're giving the reading), then ask them to shuffle the cards and to think about their question as they do so. When they've finished, ask them to cut the cards three times with their left hand, then to reassemble the pack in a different order – it doesn't matter which, provided the cards are no longer in their original sequence. The cards should now be handed to you – they are ready to be used, and should be dealt off the top of the pack. Ask the questioner to give you a general idea of the question (they don't have to supply details). Choose which tarot 'spread', or arrangement of the cards (see page 32), you will use and then deal out the cards accordingly.

An alternative way of asking your questioner to choose their cards is to get them to shuffle and cut them as usual, then to fan them out in as wide a semi-circle as you can manage. Now ask them to pick out the requisite number of cards for the spread you'll be using. As they choose each card, ask them to place it face down on the table. It is essential to keep the cards in the order in which they were chosen, so once they've been handed to you, restack them with the first card at the top. You can now deal out the cards into the spread.

Incidentally, if any cards fall on the floor while they're being shuffled, take note of them before returning them to the pack. Sometimes, a card will leap out at you and may well set the tone of the whole reading or carry an apposite message.

THE MAJOR ARCANA

These are the trump cards of the tarot, the suit of 22 cards that depict man's journey through life. In a spread drawn from the complete tarot pack, Major Arcana cards represent major events in life while Minor Arcana cards provide the details. Some spreads use only Major Arcana cards but on the whole it is best to use the entire pack because this gives a more comprehensive picture of the questioner's circumstances. In some packs, the order of the Strength and Justice cards is transposed, but this doesn't affect their meanings.

0 The Fool

The Fool represents someone who is starting out on a journey, and he's often shown standing on a high cliff, apparently poised to step into space. In other words, he is stepping out into the unknown. He appears oblivious to the peril he may be in – instead of worrying about standing on a precipice, he is confidently looking ahead to the future. The Fool is a card of new beginnings, fresh starts or changes in attitude which are embarked upon with optimism. This card is therefore usually considered to be positive, but it can occasionally show foolhardiness if surrounded by difficult cards.

Most cards depict a small dog at the Fool's heels – is it barking playfully or trying to warn his owner of imminent danger? Perhaps the new venture should be approached with a certain amount of caution because not all the facts may yet be known. This might be because the questioner is being too idealistic, is slightly foolish, or lacks willpower or discipline. Perhaps the venture requires a leap of faith?

I The Magician

This card represents new opportunities that will enable the questioner to show off their talents, demonstrating their originality and inventiveness. It's time for them to forget false modesty and to strike out in a new, dynamic and bold direction, to capitalize on their intuition, imagination and creative skills. Such a fresh start shouldn't be entered into lightly – there's often an element of trickery or doubt surrounding this card, or a difficult choice may have to be made. The Magician is particularly auspicious for business ventures and financial matters because it shows that the person has what it takes to succeed. It can also signify an important man who will enter the questioner's life, perhaps as an adviser, friend, lover or business associate. He will be extremely aware of the power he wields.

II The High Priestess

This card symbolizes dreams, knowledge and intuition. The questioner will soon be learning new lessons and gaining fresh insights into the world, provided intuition, wisdom and knowledge are used. The High Priestess can sometimes represent a man or woman, often older than the questioner, who will act as an adviser and helper. Alternatively, it may signify the questioner's own intuition and insight, telling them that they should follow their gut feelings and act on their hunches. If the questioner is worried about something, this card suggests that they're not yet in full possession of all the facts and should delay any important decisions until they have a better idea of what's involved. The

High Priestess can also represent learning – perhaps a formal period of study or a time when the person will gain knowledge through their experience of life.

III The Empress

This card is associated with fertility and abundance, so it suggests that the questioner is about to embark on a very creative and productive phase. It can appear when the questioner is soon to become a parent or when a close friend or relative is about to have a child. It's also a favourable card when the questioner has started a new love affair or is thinking of getting married because it suggests the relationship will be happy, satisfying and long-lasting. It is equally good if the questioner is thinking of moving house because it indicates that things will turn out well. This move will be particularly favourable if it brings the questioner closer to nature, perhaps because the house is in the countryside or has a large garden. The Empress is also associated with material possessions, signifying a good time to invest in beautiful, ornate or comfortable objects.

IV The Emperor

This card can signify a person or a situation. If it represents a person, then this person is authoritative and powerful, probably older than the questioner and possibly better off, too. It may be a partner or close relative who's the boss in the relationship. They can be dictatorial at times and may view life in a serious way. They may not have a great sense of humour but they can be depended upon for their steadfast nature, reliable character and worldly-wise advice. If the Emperor represents a situation, the questioner is in control of it, thanks to their willpower, logic and analytical skills. The questioner will soon be in a similar position of authority to that of the Emperor, perhaps through promotion, a new job or a rise in social status.

V The Hierophant

Also known as the Pope, the Hierophant is a powerful card that may represent a person but more usually refers to a situation. He symbolizes beliefs that are traditional, conservative and wise. If the Hierophant does represent a person, it will be someone who acts as an adviser or a counsellor in some way. If the questioner is currently experiencing problems, this card may be suggesting that they should seek professional advice or confide in a friend whose opinion and views they truly respect. If the card represents a situation, it is one in which the questioner should take the tried and tested approach. It is not a time to fly in the face of reason or to act unconventionally. Instead, the questioner should act in a sensible, honest and trustworthy way. This card can also symbolize the need to find more meaning in life, telling the questioner to look deep inside themselves to discover their spiritual values.

VI The Lovers

There are two main meanings to this card. The first, as might be expected, concerns a love affair. The Lovers can indicate an extremely strong emotional bond, such as a friendship, a working partnership, a love affair or a marriage. If the questioner has recently fallen out with their partner, this card suggests that they will be reconciled. The second meaning concerns choice – the questioner will have to make a difficult decision and usually this will involve a certain amount of sacrifice. They may be torn between what they think they should do and what they would like to do. For instance, the questioner may have to choose between two jobs, one offering financial benefits while the other promises creative satisfaction. Or they may have to balance their spiritual needs with their material ones. If so, the questioner should think very carefully about which path to follow because the outcome will be highly significant. The surrounding cards should provide more clues.

VII The Chariot

The Chariot has several meanings, but its main message concerns a struggle. This may have already taken place or it may be in the future, but it will test the questioner's character and stamina, and will require great reserves of energy. Nevertheless, the outcome will be positive and the questioner will gain a great deal, both mentally and spiritually, from the experience. This card may indicate a relationship that's undergoing a testing time, in which firm control and steady nerves are needed. Sometimes this card refers to a financial difficulty, with the questioner trying to defend their position, keep their head above water or reclaim what is rightfully theirs. Alternatively, the questioner may be considering a course of action that will require plenty of time, money and energy. Whatever the challenge, the Chariot is reassuring the questioner that they will achieve their potential and the effort will be worthwhile.

VIII Strength

Sometimes called Fortitude, this is one of the three virtues that appear in the tarot pack – the others are Justice and Temperance. This card has a very simple message – it signifies strength of purpose and of will. When it appears in a reading, it's telling the questioner that they have much more force than they realize. This may be brute strength and sheer physical stamina, in which case it's a marvellous card for someone who is sporty or athletic. It is also a good card for someone convalescing after an illness or feeling depressed, because it shows that their strength will return. Alternatively, the card may refer to mental or emotional endurance, telling the questioner they have the courage, determination, sticking power and sheer guts to be able to cope with their current challenges and eventually win through.

IX The Hermit

There is a subtle yet reassuring meaning to this card. The questioner should withdraw from life because they need to spend time in contemplation, recharging their emotional or physical batteries, or simply pondering what to do next. This card is especially appropriate if the questioner is wondering which path or direction to take in life, because they'll soon be able to reach a satisfying conclusion and things will become much better. They must stand back from the situation, keep an open mind and consider all their options. The Hermit may also be gently reminding them that they don't yet know all the facts – perhaps a new aspect of a current situation will soon be revealed. Sometimes the

Hermit suggests that the questioner need not endure a current difficulty on their own and should ask other people for their help and advice.

X The Wheel of Fortune

This is one of the most powerful cards in the whole tarot pack. It reminds us that life works in cycles and is always changing. When The Wheel of Fortune appears, it indicates that major changes are on the way. The questioner is about to enter a new cycle, a new chapter. So, if life has been difficult or unhappy lately, this will soon change. It may not happen overnight in a dramatic turn of fate, but the person's fortunes will start to rise again. The change may well come from inside the questioner rather than from an outside person or event. For instance, if they've been feeling depressed lately, it may be their attitude that alters rather than their circumstances, making them more optimistic or objective.

XI Justice

This is one of the three virtues in the Major Arcana – the others are Strength and Temperance. It's a very favourable card, indicating that the questioner is in a strong position to reach the correct decision over a current challenge or problem. They will act fairly, weigh up the pros and cons and show that they have the courage of their convictions. If the questioner is embroiled in a legal matter or a wrangle with a large institution, the outcome will be positive, provided they act in the manner suggested by this card. It sometimes appears when the questioner needs to introduce a sense of balance into their life. It's a good sign if it appears when they're about to enter a new relationship, such as a business partnership, because this will be characterized by harmony and fairness.

XII The Hanged Man

This card represents change, but it is usually an alteration in mental attitude rather than physical circumstances. The Hanged Man has two main meanings. The first is that the questioner is in some kind of limbo. They may have to bide their time while they wait for one chapter in their life to end and a new one to begin. For instance, the questioner may be in the throes of a divorce, longing for it to be completed so they can start life afresh. Whatever their current circumstances, they should be patient and use this time for careful reflection. There may also be valuable lessons to be learned. The second meaning concerns looking at life from a different perspective. This often involves viewing it from a more spiritual angle and placing less emphasis on material possessions and values. This card could appear when someone wants to give up a well-paid job and follow a vocation, in which case the sacrifices involved will be worthwhile.

XIII Death

Change is symbolized by this card, which tells the questioner that the old order will give way to the new. It's the end of an era. They're being given the opportunity to make a fresh start, to embark on a new phase in their life and to put the past behind them. For instance, it may be the end of a relationship, a job or a way of life and, although this

will be painful at the time, the questioner will eventually realize it was a blessing in disguise. This card is also favourable if the questioner is trying to transform their life, perhaps by going out on a limb in some way. Although the changes may be hard to deal with at first, the questioner can turn them into something positive.

XIV Temperance

This is one of the three virtues to appear in the tarot pack – the others are Justice and Strength. It has several meanings. The first is that the questioner is being urged to be moderate and to find a balance when dealing with problems. They must find a happy medium and avoid adopting an extreme point of view. Secondly, the questioner should come to terms with the past in some way in order to have a happier or more fulfilling future. Another meaning is that the questioner should use their innate talents in order to reach their goals. The fourth meaning is that the questioner should adopt a more prudent financial approach, especially if they've been extravagant lately or soon will be. The fifth meaning is that they should adopt a more healthy way of life, especially if they eat or drink too much. Finally, if they've been working hard or finding life an uphill struggle, this difficult phase will soon end.

XV The Devil

This card is all about being enslaved to something or someone. It could be an idea, a relationship, a way of life, an unsatisfactory job, a bad habit or a self-destructive attitude. This represents a trap for the questioner, yet it's of their own making and, even though they may imagine they can't escape from it, there is a way out if they can only see it. Very often this means they should stop blaming other people for their misfortunes and start to study their own involvement in whatever has gone wrong. This may be neither easy nor comfortable, yet the questioner will remain enslaved to the difficult situation until they break the psychological or emotional chains that bind them to it. Sometimes the card can suggest that someone is making trouble behind the questioner's back, in which case they should follow their conscience and ensure they don't act in any way that will cause further problems. Finally, this card can predict that the questioner will soon enjoy a passionate, raunchy and sexy relationship.

XVI The Tower

Change is on the horizon. A dramatic turn of fate is about to enter the questioner's life and it may strike like a bolt from the blue. This may be an alteration to the questioner's circumstances, or it might be a change in their attitude. It will be a blow to their ego, so they may lose face, feel embarrassed or have to admit that they're wrong in some way. Although this experience may be unpleasant at the time, once the dust has settled the questioner will be pleased that the change happened and may also feel proud of the way they've coped. Sometimes this card appears when the questioner is discovering the truth about someone in their life. This person may let them down badly or reveal a new, unpleasant, side to their character. Although the questioner will be unhappy about this at the time, eventually they will realize that they had a lucky escape.

XVII The Star

One of the most fortunate cards of the tarot, the Star has a very simple message. It's the wish card, telling the questioner that a dream is about to be realized or a particular area of their life will soon bring them fulfilment and happiness. They must be positive, have hope and trust that all will be well. If the questioner has recently been ill, unhappy or depressed, the Star is reassuring them that they will soon feel much better. It brings equally good news if the questioner is awaiting the results of medical tests, an exam result, a job interview or anything else that's worrying them. This card can also represent the questioner's creativity and artistic abilities, suggesting they can use these talents in new ways that will bring them immense satisfaction. In addition, it's an excellent card to appear when a questioner is embarking on a new relationship, because it shows that happy experiences and opportunities are on the way.

XVIII The Moon

Things are not what they seem. The Moon gently warns that, although everything may seem to be peaceful on the surface, there is an undercurrent of deceit, trickery or misunderstanding. Perhaps someone is duping the questioner, or they might be deceiving themselves in some way. For instance, they may be putting a brave face on a relationship that is secretly causing them sadness or anger. Alternatively, they may be the victim of hidden fears that are preventing them from reaching their full emotional or creative potential. If so, they must confront these fears and take control of them. This card can also indicate a muddle in which messages go astray, someone doesn't tell the truth or the questioner is at cross-purposes with someone. If they're about to go on a journey, they should double-check all the arrangements to avoid last-minute hitches.

XIX The Sun

The Sun is one of the most happy and positive cards in the tarot. It tells the questioner that joy, happiness and contentment will soon be theirs. This may refer to something that they already know about or it may be something that will happen unexpectedly. Either way, life will soon become very happy indeed and the outlook will be extremely positive. If the questioner has been going through a miserable or sticky patch, all that will soon change and they'll have fresh hope and a new reason for living. This may come from inside themselves, or from someone or something else. The Sun is a particularly auspicious card where the emotions are concerned, because it can show that a new love is on the way or that a current relationship will bring increased happiness. It also symbolizes children. The questioner may draw closer to a child they already know, there might be good news about a child or they could soon hear of the birth of a child.

XX Judgement

Sometimes called the Angel, this card has a very simple but profound meaning – a second chance. The questioner is being offered a spiritual rebirth, the opportunity to review recent events and actions and to offer forgiveness or make amends. They are being urged to analyse their actions, to study their failings, faults and weaknesses carefully so they can learn many lessons about themselves. This is particularly apt if the questioner is harbouring a grudge or feeling bitter about an episode from their past. They don't have to forget, but perhaps it's now time to forgive? This card can also symbolize the end of an era, so the questioner can take stock of where they stand, congratulate themselves on their past efforts and then look eagerly to the future. If they are working hard on a project, their efforts will be rewarded. This may mean promotion, a job offer or something more abstract, such as a new-found confidence in themselves.

XXI The World

Previous hard work or sacrifices bring rich rewards when this card appears. Its simple message concerns achievement, praise and satisfaction. Like so many other tarot cards, the World is all about change. It describes reaching the end of one satisfactory era and moving on to the next. If the questioner has been wondering whether to change jobs or move house, the World gives them the green light. Sometimes this card appears when the questioner is about to give birth or when their grown-up children will soon leave home, in which case it represents the start of an enjoyable and exciting new phase. This card can also indicate travel, or even emigration, whether this is planned at the time of the reading or not. If the questioner is thinking of going on holiday, this card suggests they should travel to somewhere they've never been before, especially if it's exotic or steeped in history or culture.

THE MINOR ARCANA

The Minor Arcana consists of 56 cards, divided into the four suits of Cups, Wands, Pentacles and Swords. Each suit has four court cards – the Page, the Knight, the Queen and the King. Minor Arcana cards can give very specific information about events and circumstances. The interpretations have been arranged numerically, to help you understand and remember how the influences of each number are coloured by each of the suits.

Cups

Cups are connected with deep emotions, such as happiness, friendship, love and marriage. They are also associated with material goods, possessions and belongings. Cups are linked with the Water signs of Cancer, Scorpio and Pisces.

Wands

Wands are connected with energy and ambition, with enterprise, growth and progress. They're also associated with travel, negotiations and the ability to be creative with words. Wands are linked with the Fire signs of Aries, Leo and Sagittarius.

Pentacles

Pentacles are linked with material matters, such as money, status and property, and anything else that the questioner really values in life. They are also associated with business and with the foundations on which plans can be turned into reality. Pentacles are allied with the Earth signs of Taurus, Virgo and Capricorn.

Swords

Swords are associated with the mind, and therefore with ideas and worries. They are also connected with action and travel, both mental and physical. Swords are double-edged, so this suit is linked with problems, arguments, set-backs, delays, disappointments, loss and separation. They are also connected with professional people who can give advice, such as lawyers, doctors, accountants and so on. Swords have ties with the Air signs of Gemini, Libra and Aquarius.

THE ACES

One is the number of creative potential, power, energy and originality. Therefore, the Aces suggest new beginnings and fresh starts, heralding a time when the questioner can seize the initiative and take action. Life will become extremely busy and exciting.

Ace of Cups

The questioner is about to embark either on a new relationship or a fresh chapter in an existing partnership. This could be a deep love or it may be an enriching friendship, and it will bring much happiness and plenty of emotional fulfilment. It may also have spiritual overtones, perhaps because the person concerned will give the questioner valuable advice. This card is connected with abundance and fertility, so it can foretell the birth of a child or the start of an enjoyably creative and artistic phase.

Ace of Wands

This is a particularly auspicious card when the questioner is thinking of starting a new enterprise or project that will involve plenty of hard work. It's a good time in which to further aims and ambitions by taking the initiative and grasping opportunities as they arise. This card can symbolize an important letter, document or phone call, a forthcoming adventure or an enjoyable holiday. It can also represent the birth of a marvellous idea and the dawn of a more spiritual phase in the questioner's life.

Ace of Pentacles

The questioner is being urged to get a new business venture off the ground or to begin any scheme or idea that means a lot to them. This might be moving to a new house or improving their current home, or something else that will boost their sense of self-esteem. Money is usually on the horizon when this card appears, and it may arrive in the form of a gift, a windfall, a win or a pay rise. A traditional meaning is the gift of a ring – is a wedding in the offing?

Ace of Swords

The questioner is about to become involved in something that will really engross them. It could be a high-powered job that takes up all their time, a love affair that totally overwhelms them or a difficulty or challenge that demands all their mental energy if they're to combat and overcome it. Any new venture or enterprise should be thought through carefully before it's put into practice, in case the questioner has overlooked vital details.

THE TWOS

Twos represent partnerships and relationships. They are also the number of balance, harmony, co-operation and choice. After the power and energy of Aces, Twos give the questioner the chance to restore balance and reduce conflict.

Two of Cups

The literal meaning of this card is two hearts, so it refers to a particular relationship. It's an excellent card if the questioner has chosen to go into partnership with someone, or will soon have an important meeting with them, for whatever reason. It may foretell a new friendship, love affair, engagement or marriage. Alternatively, it can signify the signing of a contract – anything from a marriage licence to a rental agreement.

A set of Italian tarocchi cards from the late nineteenth century, showing a mixture of Major Arcana and Minor Arcana cards.

Two of Wands

This represents someone who knows what they're doing and who is being given a tremendous opportunity. This may be the questioner or a person they'll soon be dealing with. Either way, this is someone who knows they're in a strong position and acts accordingly. There could be a business partnership on the way, or the questioner may soon start negotiating over a property deal.

Two of Pentacles

There's a balancing act whenever this card appears. It may be difficult for the questioner to make ends meet or they may find that no sooner does the money come in than it goes out again. Alternatively, the questioner will be juggling their time or energy in some way, perhaps through family ties or extra work. Even though the going may be tough, if the questioner can draw on their reserves of patience and endurance, everything will work out well.

Two of Swords

Stalemate! The questioner is stuck in a situation in which there appears to be no leeway. They can't progress, yet it seems they can't escape either. This card often appears after the questioner has had a flaming row, when they're caught in a legal impasse, or when they're so frightened by the prospect of something that they feel incapable of doing anything about it. However, until they can confront their fear they will be unable to take action and will remain trapped.

THE THREES

Three is the number of creativity, energy, enthusiasm, action, growth and expansion. The questioner can now enjoy the results of the partnerships that were started during the previous phase, or the problems that were resolved.

Three of Cups

Traditionally, this card means a joyful celebration, so it's an excellent omen for a forthcoming party or reception. Alternatively, it signifies the end of a problem. A happy outcome may not occur automatically because the questioner will have to work hard for it, but they can rest assured that, if they do this, everything will turn out for the best. This is also a favourable card if the questioner has been ill or sad because it indicates a turn in their fortunes.

Three of Wands

The questioner is in an excellent position, and able to survey what's going on around them and make intelligent decisions based on that knowledge. It's a good time for them to communicate their ideas and suggestions, either verbally or in writing. There's a feeling of movement about this card, so even though the questioner has already put in a lot of effort and made progress, they can't afford to rest on their laurels for long because they still have a great deal to accomplish.

Three of Pentacles

Hard work will bring results when this card appears. It shows that the questioner has already carried out the groundwork of a scheme or project connected with material matters, property or business, and they are now ready to work on the finer details. If they do so, they can expect rewards and acclaim for their efforts. This might be a financial reward or it could be a deep sense of satisfaction and pride.

Three of Swords

A stressful card, suggesting emotional difficulties or sorrow. This could be the end of a relationship, a sense of betrayal caused by infidelity, a breakdown in communications, a separation or a bitter argument. Sometimes this card denotes an illness or medical procedure – anything from an injection to an operation. The problems will be resolved and out of bad will come good, especially if the questioner is honest with themselves about what exactly is wrong.

THE FOURS

This is the number of structure, logic, order, stability and reason. The Fours can bring a sense of contentment to the questioner or they might be a cause of dissatisfaction and restlessness.

Four of Cups

A sense of discontentment and boredom is associated with this card. The questioner is stuck in a rut or is so trapped by routine that life has ceased to hold any pleasure or excitement. Yet life is not nearly as dreary or mundane as the questioner imagines, because there's an opportunity in store. However, they must be far-sighted enough to recognize it – it may appear in an unexpected way or the questioner may have to broaden their outlook on life before they can see what is being offered to them.

Four of Wands

This is a lovely card to appear in a spread because it signifies success, contentment and achievement after a period of hard work. If the questioner has been pulling out all the stops in a business or career matter, they will earn the respect of others, will boost their self-confidence and may be rewarded with a pay rise or promotion. This card can also mean that the questioner will soon be increasing their sense of emotional security and putting down roots, perhaps literally by creating a garden or moving house.

Four of Pentacles

A sense of security is denoted by this card. It could be financial or it could be physical, but it'll bring the questioner a great deal of happiness and satisfaction. However, this card carries a warning, because it's advising them not to place too much importance on the things they own. Otherwise, they may become bogged down in materialistic values, be complacent or be reluctant to take chances because of the risks involved. They may grow suspicious of other people's motives or become greedy, mercenary and miserly.

Four of Swords

A period of hard work will be followed by a time of rest and relaxation. This card is telling the questioner that they've just successfully completed something important – it could be a work project, a difficult negotiation or a testing time – and they now deserve a breather. This may be a relaxing holiday, convalescence after an illness or operation, or a time when the questioner can take life easy and recharge their batteries.

THE FIVES

Five is the number of change, uncertainty and versatility. In the tarot, unlike numerology, it can also represent a sense of loss and regret.

Five of Cups

A sense of disappointment, regret, loss or even grief accompanies this card. It often appears when a relationship has come to an end or when there's an enforced separation between the questioner and a loved one. The questioner may find it hard to contemplate the future with much optimism or may be completely wrapped up in their misery. Instead of focusing on what they've lost, the questioner needs to concentrate on what still remains, and to make the most of it.

Five of Wands

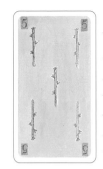

The questioner needs to draw on their reserves of patience and strength in order to deal with a difficult situation or cope with an irritating phase when nothing goes according to plan. Business deals may be put on hold or be subject to delays, with the questioner unable to do anything to help the situation, and communications will be fraught with difficulties. Travel plans may be affected, so the questioner should make sure that all the arrangements have been taken care of and nothing has been left to chance or postponed until the last minute.

Five of Pentacles

A difficult card, this indicates that the questioner is about to enter a temporary phase when something they truly value will be put in jeopardy. Money might be tight, a partner will be difficult or they may have doubts about a spiritual or religious belief. Sometimes they may view life from a very materialistic angle. Although this bleak patch will soon be over, it won't be very pleasant while it lasts. Things look bad but they may not be as grim as they seem, provided the questioner keeps track of details and doesn't let things slide.

Five of Swords

It may be time for the questioner to admit defeat over something, especially if it seems they're banging their heads against a brick wall. They should swallow their pride, accept their limitations and then concentrate on something at which they will succeed. This may involve a significant change of attitude or a climb-down, yet this will be in the questioner's best interests in the long run. The surrounding cards will show whether this change of heart is easily made.

THE SIXES

Six is the number of balance, harmony, service and a love of the home and family.

Six of Cups

This card has two main meanings. The first suggests that someone or something from the questioner's past will return in a way that will help to create their future. For instance, a long-lost friend may get in touch and play a big role in their life or an old skill may stand them in good stead. The second meaning tells the questioner that they're living too much in the past, or are feeling a nostalgia that is quite unfounded or misplaced.

Six of Wands

Success and achievement are the meanings of this card. It often appears when the questioner has been working hard to finish a job or to pull off a deal, and it indicates that they will soon reap the rewards of all their efforts. Not only will they be pleased with themselves but other people will also appreciate what they've done. Therefore, this card can be an indication of a forthcoming promotion or improved job prospects.

Six of Pentacles

Good financial news is on the way. If the questioner is currently owed money, this card suggests that the debt will be paid. It can also appear when the questioner is about to inherit some money or property, or when someone is going to make them a lavish gift of some sort. Alternatively, the questioner will feel generous and benevolent, and will gladly share their good fortune with their friends and loved ones.

Six of Swords

Current problems will be overcome and present difficulties will end. Even if things seem black at

the moment, the questioner will soon see the light at the end of the tunnel. Tension and stress will ease, leaving the questioner feeling much more peaceful and relaxed. This card can also sometimes indicate a journey or a move to more pleasing and harmonious surroundings.

THE SEVENS

Seven is the number of wisdom, spirituality, philosophy and psychic abilities. Many cycles in nature correspond to the number seven – there are seven days of the week and seven ages of man and all the cells in our bodies renew themselves every seven years. Therefore, seven can indicate the end of a cycle.

Seven of Cups

This card has fabulous potential and indicates great creative and imaginative gifts. It also shows that the questioner will soon be spoilt for choice. They'll be presented with several offers or courses of action, but they should choose wisely because some of these offers will not be as promising or profitable as they seem. Though some of the choices could be worthless, one will bring the questioner a marvellous opportunity. But which?

Seven of Wands

If the questioner is currently facing a difficult challenge or struggle, or some form of opposition to a current scheme, they'll succeed if they can use their willpower, courage and determination. This won't be easy and they aren't out of the woods yet, but they will win in the end. If the questioner is considering taking a particular course of action, this card is saying to go ahead.

Seven of Pentacles

The questioner has been working hard and has good reason to feel satisfied with all their efforts.

However, even though they may deserve a break, they should not feel complacent because there is still a long way to go before they can reach their goal. This card is telling them that they need to take stock of how much they've achieved so far and what they have yet to accomplish.

Seven of Swords

A difficult card, this indicates that the questioner longs to escape from an unpleasant situation. It may involve being evasive or economical with the truth, cutting their losses or having to lose face in some way. It's a time for using their intelligence, charm, diplomacy and, possibly, guile. Sometimes this card warns that someone will take advantage of the questioner by ripping them off or deceiving them, so they should be on their guard. Occasionally, it may mean it's the questioner who's being dishonest.

THE EIGHTS

Eight is the number of power, business, material success and worldly prosperity. It is one of the most powerful numbers of all and in the tarot it symbolizes regeneration and various changes for the better.

Eight of Cups

There are changes on the way in a relationship. This could be a romantic link, a business alliance or a friendship that has reached a natural ending. The questioner feels that it's time to move on to pastures new, even though this may involve making painful decisions and having to hurt someone they care about. In fact, this card marks the end of one chapter in the questioner's life and the start of a new one; an ending will lead on to a beginning.

Eight of Wands

Life is about to become very busy and lively. There's a strong sense of action and movement which may be physical, with the questioner doing some travelling or moving house, or it could be mental, perhaps through an extremely busy phase at work. Sometimes this card symbolizes a lucky break that appears to come out of the blue, although actually it's the questioner's hard work that has attracted this opportunity.

Eight of Pentacles

The questioner should make the most of their potential and could turn particular talents into money. This might be pin-money or it could be the beginning of a satisfying career that draws on their creative or artistic abilities. The card is certainly saying that, provided the questioner is prepared to expend a lot of effort and practical ability, they'll be able to build up a career that will be emotionally and financially satisfying.

Eight of Swords

The questioner is trapped in a difficult situation and feels that there's no escape. In fact, they're paralysed by their own fears and are not nearly as restricted as they imagine. The problems they face are not as bad or insoluble as they think but they're too frightened or upset to consider them rationally. However, they will soon see the way forward and will be able to break free from these limiting circumstances.

THE NINES

Nine is the number of brotherly love, humanitarian concerns and perfection. Both the Nine of Cups and the Nine of Pentacles are fortunate, hinting that completion is just around the corner, but the Nine of Wands and Nine of Swords are both rather miserable cards.

Nine of Cups

The 'wish' card of the Minor Arcana, this promises physical and emotional contentment and stability. The questioner's cherished wish or dream will finally be realized, bringing them immense emotional, material and physical satisfaction. It is a particularly auspicious card if the questioner will soon become engaged, get married or move in with someone, or is about to begin a new business venture. It can also indicate the start of a very sensuous love affair.

Nine of Wands

The questioner should hold on to their current assets and circumstances because they may soon be faced by a lot of demands for their time or money. For instance, they should conserve their energies and horde their cash, and understand that this is not a good time to make major changes to their life such as moving house or changing jobs. In the meantime, they should keep calm, relying on their strength of character and their determination to succeed.

Nine of Pentacles

Material security and physical comfort are on the horizon, and the questioner will experience a deep sense of well-being and contentment. This is a particularly favourable card if the questioner is currently in the throes of moving house or has been undergoing domestic upheavals, because it's telling them that much happier times are just around the corner.

Nine of Swords

The traditional meaning of this card is 'sleepless nights', because the questioner is feeling frightened, miserable or depressed about something. This may be affecting their sleep or health but, although these fears are very real, they may not

have much bearing on reality. In fact, the questioner may be in a much better position than they imagine, as they will soon realize if they can only face the facts and start to deal with them.

THE TENS

Ten is the number of completion, the end of one cycle and the beginning of the next, in which we carry with us the knowledge that we've gained in the previous cycle. The Ten of Cups and the Ten of Pentacles both show the height of fulfilment, while the Ten of Wands and Ten of Swords both indicate difficulties that can be surmounted.

Ten of Cups

This card symbolizes lasting happiness and contentment, especially at home or among the family. It tells the questioner that they will soon achieve their desires and have their dearest wishes granted. They will be surrounded by a great deal of love and will also be able to show it to other people. This is a wonderful card if the questioner is about to get married or move in with someone.

Ten of Wands

The Ten of Wands indicates that the questioner is shouldering a big burden or coping with a lot of responsibility which is wearing them down. The load may be material, physical or emotional, but it is taking its toll on the questioner. However, it may be that this burden is self-imposed, perhaps because they've taken on too much at once or because they're driving themselves into the ground trying to live up to their own high expectations. The card is suggesting that the burden can be lifted or the problem resolved.

Ten of Pentacles

This card symbolizes the completion of something that will bring the questioner abundance, personal satisfaction and a strong sense of emotional and material security. They may also experience a happy and fulfilling home life, perhaps with all their family gathered around them. This is an excellent card if the questioner will soon be moving house or is about to start a family.

Ten of Swords

There will be a complete ending in a particular area of the questioner's life. This might be an attitude of mind, a relationship or a physical situation. There is usually a sense of inevitability about this ending and, although it may be accompanied by worry, sadness or a sense of betrayal, the questioner will soon realize that, having hit rock bottom, the only way to go now is up. They can learn from experience and approach the future with hope and optimism.

THE PAGES

The first of the court cards, Pages can denote either a situation or a person in the questioner's life. If a situation, it's one that is just beginning. If a person, it's usually a child, or a new aspect of someone's personality. Occasionally, it is someone who is entering or leaving the questioner's life, or who no longer occupies the important place in the questioner's heart that they once did.

Page of Cups

If this card represents a person in the questioner's life, they are kind, loving and thoughtful. They may be studious or creative, and will bring comfort to the questioner. If it represents a situation, it's the beginning of a course of study or contemplation in which the questioner will view life from a spiritual angle. It can also mean that a new venture will turn out well.

Page of Wands

This card can symbolize the start of an exciting new adventure, such as a wonderful holiday or an enjoyable journey. It can also mean that some important news is on the way. If the card represents a person, it's someone who is enthusiastic, lively and high-spirited.

Page of Pentacles

If this card represents a situation, it usually indicates a small improvement in the questioner's finances. There may also be the chance to make some money but this will involve plenty of hard work. When the card symbolizes a person, it's someone who is trustworthy, practical, orderly, responsible and efficient. They may have an old head on young shoulders.

Page of Swords

An important document, contract or letter could be on the way but the questioner should check it through carefully as it may contain accidental or deliberate mistakes. Alternatively, someone may be gossip-mongering or doing some double-dealing. If the card represents a person, they're very clever, calculating, strong-willed and rather aloof. They might also be aggressive.

THE KNIGHTS

Knights represent either a situation or a person. If a situation, it's one that involves movement and action. If a person, it's either someone who is relatively young or who's older but isn't particularly important to the questioner.

Knight of Cups

When it represents a situation, this card suggests that new opportunities will soon arrive. They'll probably be connected with artistic ventures, an emotional matter or a spiritual quest of some sort. If the card symbolizes a person, it's probably a man who is sensitive, friendly and fond of the questioner. He may be creative and idealistic but is not known for his practical attitude to life.

Knight of Wands

Travel is indicated, especially if it takes the questioner far afield – they may move house or even emigrate. Usually this will be backed up by other cards that symbolize great changes. Alternatively, there may be visitors from another country. If the card represents a person, it's someone who is generous, popular, sociable and outgoing. They can be unpredictable at times and are full of ideas that don't always come to anything. Nevertheless, they are good fun to be around. They may also be extremely chatty.

Knight of Pentacles

If a situation has been dragging on for a long time or has looked like a lost cause, this card suggests that it will soon be resolved. When this card represents a person, it's someone who is reliable, responsible, trustworthy and a hard worker. They don't like taking risks and this cautious approach may sometimes irritate the questioner, who wishes they were less pragmatic.

Knight of Swords

When this card represents a situation, it's one that starts quickly, gallops along and then comes to an end just as rapidly. The questioner may make quick decisions or swift changes in their life. When the card represents a person, it's someone who loves taking action. They are clever, articulate, ambitious and have a good career. However, they can cause trouble because their impatience means they rush in where angels fear to tread.

THE QUEENS

The Queens represent women who are important to the questioner. Alternatively, they symbolize an aspect of the questioner's personality that is significant at the time of the reading. This applies to men as well as women.

Queen of Cups

This woman is very kind, warm and gentle. She is quite sensuous and may even be an earth mother, perhaps surrounded by a brood of happy children or loving friends. She is always most content when she's in her own home. There is something other-worldly about her because she's in touch with the more spiritual aspects of life and probably also because she's strongly intuitive and psychic. She will give the questioner support and affection.

Queen of Wands

This is a very versatile lady. Not only is she able to run her home efficiently, but she also has plenty of outside interests. She's a good hostess and people enjoy being with her because she's so lively, warm-hearted and fascinating to talk to. She's interested in other people and, as a result, is often the first person to hear people's tales of woe. Despite being very good-natured she will soon set anyone straight if they try to take advantage of her.

Queen of Pentacles

Here is a woman who is good at business. She is capable, reliable and probably doesn't suffer fools gladly. Her work may involve her in financial matters, in property deals or with the land. She works very hard and enjoys the material comforts that money brings. She finds it difficult to show her emotions but her family are important to her and she will quickly come to their support.

Queen of Swords

Rather serious and solemn, this woman probably lives alone and has become practised at looking after herself without asking other people for help. She might be rather lonely and has had her fair share of troubles, which she's borne with strength and patience. However, good times will return for her. If the questioner is going through a bad patch, this card is telling them to adopt the stoic attitude of the Queen of Swords.

THE KINGS

These cards represent either important men to the questioner at the time of the reading or an aspect of their own personality that they need to develop or control. This applies to women as well as men. Sometimes, these cards can symbolize a young man who has a very mature attitude to life.

King of Cups

This man is kind and considerate, although at times he may feel uncomfortable about showing this sensitive side of his personality. He is probably a professional and commands plenty of respect, but not a lot of affection. As a result, this card may be telling the questioner that they need to get more in touch with their feelings.

King of Wands

The King of Wands is friendly and chatty and has a great sense of humour. His honest and conscientious approach to life makes him popular and highly respected. He's at his best when dreaming up good ideas and money-making schemes, but he's not so hot when it comes to putting these ideas into practice and following them through. He's good at his job but may try to offload work on to other people. It may be difficult for him to commit himself emotionally.

King of Pentacles

The King of Pentacles is extremely reliable and always honours his word. He's probably a successful businessman and is generous with his cash. This man is very contented with his life and, if he represents a part of the questioner's personality that needs to be developed, it may be the ability to be happy with their lot. In other words, they should count their blessings and be thankful for the good things in their life.

King of Swords

The man represented by this card is pretty powerful. He is intelligent, logical and rational; he has a strict moral code and a strong air of authority. He's able to judge situations clearly. He is a good friend in a crisis, so this card may be telling the questioner to seek professional advice, to rely on their own strength of character or to keep their distance from current problems in order to cope with them objectively.

INTERPRETING THE TAROT

A spread is the pattern in which the cards are laid out, and also the order in which they fall when dealt out. There are many tarot spreads to choose from, some of which help you to gain a general picture of someone's life and some of which are much more specific, allowing you to focus on a particular problem or question. This chapter contains three spreads, all of which perform different functions, and there is also advice on how to invent your own spreads. The spreads given in the cartomancy chapter can be used for tarot readings, and vice versa, although you may have to make a few adaptations.

GUIDELINES

Before you begin to interpret the individual cards in a spread, examine the overall balance of cards to get a general flavour of the reading. Are there more Major Arcana cards than you would statistically expect? (A normal ratio is three Minor Arcana cards to every Major Arcana card.) Is there an emphasis on one of the Minor Arcana suits? All of these have their own significance and will give an extra depth to your reading. For instance, when two or more court cards appear in a reading, they mean that the questioner is currently being influenced by other people. A preponderance of Major Arcana cards indicates that matters are out of the questioner's hands, while an emphasis on Minor Arcana cards means that the questioner is in control of the situation. Do most of the cards have positive meanings, suggesting that things are going well for the questioner? Are they all about change? Or are there several of the more difficult cards, such as the Tower and the Moon? If there are two or more cards of a number, bear in mind its basic meaning when giving your interpretation. For instance, if there are three Fives, you should remember that Five is the number of change, uncertainty and, possibly, regret.

Lack of space means the interpretations given for each spread are very brief and can only describe the essence of each card's meaning. However, you can expand on these interpretations when you do a reading.

Occasionally, the tarot appears to have a will of its own. Although the cards are dealt out to answer a specific question, they'll ignore it and will talk about something else. For instance, if the questioner wants to know about their career, the cards may describe their love life. If so, explain what's happening and read the cards' message, then suggest that the questioner shuffles the cards and asks their original question again.

An illustration from a nineteenth-century French magazine

CONSEQUENCES SPREAD

This is an excellent spread when the questioner has to make a difficult choice because it offers them a good overview of their current situation and their future potential. Make sure the questioner phrases their question in a simple way that can be answered with 'yes' or 'no'. Questions like 'Will my forthcoming holiday be cancelled or will it go ahead?' are confusing – if the answer is 'yes', does it mean yes, the holiday will be cancelled or yes, it will go ahead? It would be better to ask, 'Will I soon be going on holiday?'

Ask the questioner to shuffle and cut the cards in the usual way, and then to hand them to you. Deal them into the pattern shown here. Sometimes the cards will give you a very clear-cut answer and at other times they'll be much harder to interpret. If the 'outcome card' (the last one to be dealt, which can often specify the outcome) seems to contradict the rest of the spread, you can draw another card from the top of the discard pile and see if that clarifies the situation. If it only muddies the waters further, you may decide that the outcome is not yet settled. You could try the reading again on another day or phrase the question in a different way.

Here, the questioner wanted to know if she should develop a new work project that would take her career in a completely different direction. The tarot's response was very definite and positive, as the interpretation below shows. It contained five cards from the Major Arcana and only two from the Minor Arcana, investing the reading with extra significance. It seems that there will be something fated about the questioner's decision, and much of it is out of her hands.

CARD CATEGORIES

1 **The questioner's current circumstances**

2 **Immediate prospects**

3 **Past actions**

4 **Future actions**

5 **The questioner's potential**

6 **Outside influences**

7 **Outcome/summary of situation**

INTERPRETATION OF EXAMPLE

1 Page of Pentacles
The questioner is currently in a good financial position.

2 Five of Wands
She will soon face a challenge that she will surmount.

3 The Tower
There have been significant changes for the better.

4 The Lovers
The questioner will have to make a choice that involves a sacrifice or moral dilemma.

5 Strength
Whatever happens, the questioner has the willpower and inner strength to succeed.

6 The Magician
Someone in an influential position will be a great help to the questioner.

7 Justice
A card of harmony and balance – the outcome will be extremely favourable.

PAGE OF PENTACLES

1

2

THE TOWER

3

JUSTICE

7

THE LOVERS

4

THE MAGICIAN

6

STRENGTH

5

CELTIC CROSS SPREAD

This is one of the most popular tarot spreads of all because it gives an excellent overview of the questioner's situation. Use it to answer a specific question or simply to see where the questioner stands at the time of the reading. You can use either the whole tarot pack for this spread or only the 22 cards of the Major Arcana.

The following spread was given for a questioner who wanted to gain an overall picture of his life because he felt that his marriage was on the rocks. The cards certainly picked up on this theme, since they all dealt with sadness and endings, yet ultimately they carried a positive message. There was a good balance of Major and Minor Arcana cards, but the fact that the questioner drew two of the most stressful cards in the pack (The Tower and the Ten of Swords) confirmed his worst fears for the marriage. When the cards were dealt out again, after a good shuffle,

seven of them reappeared in virtually the same positions as before. The presence of two court cards indicates the influence of other people over the questioner – these were obviously his family.

CARD CATEGORIES

1 **The questioner's current circumstances**

2 **Current influences**

3 **Future influences**

4 **Future events**

5 **Past influences**

6 **Past events**

7 **The questioner's feelings**

8 **Outside influences**

9 **The questioner's hopes and fears**

10 **The outcome/resolution**

INTERPRETATION OF EXAMPLE

1 Queen of Wands
A warm, friendly and businesslike woman – the questioner's wife.

2 Page of Pentacles
This card can represent friends but here it symbolizes the questioner's young daughters.

3 Three of Cups
There will be a happy outcome to a problem if the questioner is prepared to work hard for it.

4 Eight of Cups
This card symbolizes the questioner's dissatisfaction with

his life and reflects his sense that his marriage has reached a natural ending.

5 The World
He has reached the end of a satisfying cycle in his life and is now ready to begin another.

6 Ten of Swords
Another ending, although this time it is accompanied by sadness, regret and pain.

7 The Magician
This card places the questioner in an ideal position to begin a fresh chapter in his life.

8 Eight of Wands
Professional commitments are going to keep the questioner very busy, and could even involve some travel.

9 The Tower
Major changes and upheavals are in store, as the questioner feared, and matters may be taken out of his hands.

10 The Chariot
It will be a very testing time for the questioner, but this card suggests that he will survive and the marital break-up will lead to new opportunities.

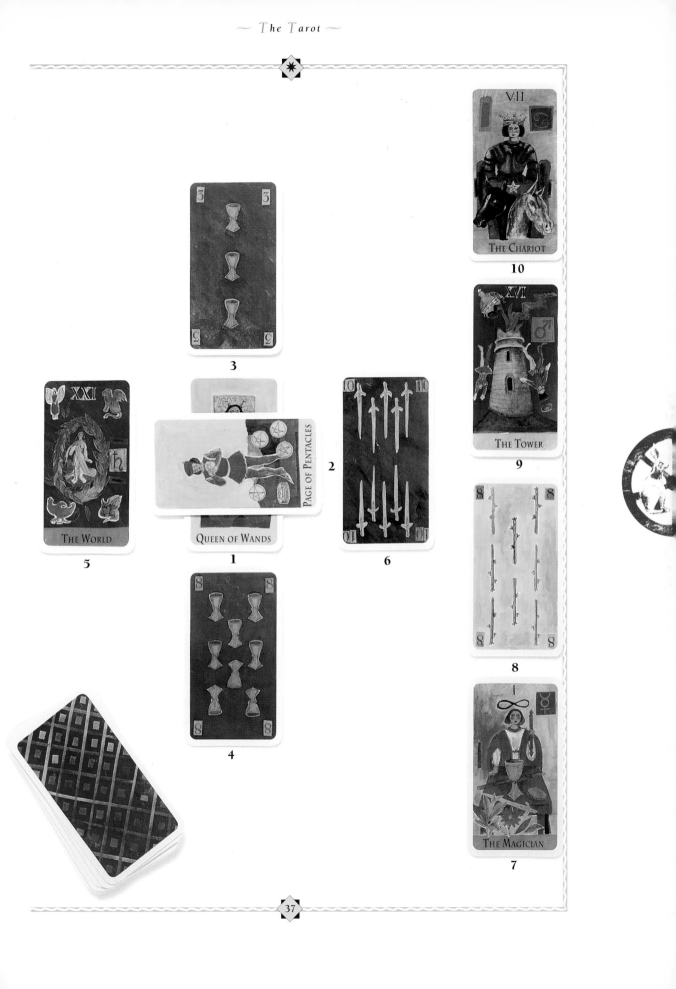

3

10
THE CHARIOT

XVI
THE TOWER
9

2

PAGE OF PENTACLES

QUEEN OF WANDS
1

6

8

THE WORLD
5

4

7
THE MAGICIAN

THE HOROSCOPE SPREAD

This is an invaluable spread for looking closely at the different areas of someone's life. It's called the Horoscope Spread because the meaning of the 12 categories is very similar to that of the 12 houses (areas of life) of the horoscope. You can use this spread to gain a general picture of someone's circumstances at the time of the reading or as a guide to their life over the coming year, with the first card representing the current month, the second card the following month, and so on.

The example shown here only uses the 22 cards of the Major Arcana, which is particularly suited to this spread, but the complete pack of 78 cards gives equally good results. The questioner wanted a guide to the state of her life at the time of this reading.

After the questioner has shuffled and cut the cards in the usual way, deal them out in the pattern shown here. Note that the first card is on the left and the cards run clockwise in a circle. Interpret each card in the light of its category. For instance, in this spread the Moon represents personal matters, meaning that the questioner must take care not to be deceived – or to deceive herself – over a personal situation or problem.

THE MOON

1

TEMPERANCE

2

THE HANGED MAN

12

JUDGEMENT

11

CARD CATEGORIES

1 **Personal matters**

2 **Possessions, things the questioner values**

3 **Day-to-day activities, communications**

4 **Home and family**

5 **Creativity, lovers, children, pleasure**

6 **Health and work**

7 **Relationships**

8 **Joint money matters, sex**

9 **Education, challenges**

10 **Career, goals, ambitions, reputation**

11 **Hobbies, friends, hopes for the future**

12 **Secrets, fears, psychic ability**

THE FOOL

3

STRENGTH

4

JUSTICE

5

DEATH

6

THE HIEROPHANT

10

THE LOVERS

9

THE SUN

8

THE WORLD

7

INTERPRETATION OF EXAMPLE

1 The Moon
There is an element of trickery or deception in the questioner's personal life.

2 Temperance
She should be moderate with her money and not waste it on fripperies.

3 The Fool
Important changes are on the way in her daily routine.

4 Strength
Certain members of the family will rely on her, and she will be able to help them.

5 Justice
The questioner will enjoy a very balanced and harmonious loving relationship.

6 Death
She needs to take more care of her health.

7 The World
A relationship will bring her immense opportunities.

8 The Sun
Joint money matters will bring dividends. A sexual relationship will be enjoyable.

9 The Lovers
Her conscience or beliefs will be tested. She should trust her instincts.

10 The Hierophant
The questioner should take the conventional route in her career or business life.

11 Judgement
The questioner should revise her opinion of a friend and stop bearing a grudge.

12 The Hanged Man
She must confront her fears and look at them from a new angle.

INVENTING YOUR OWN SPREADS

Once you're familiar with the way the tarot works, you can create spreads to answer specific questions that you want to raise. Keep a note of each one's accuracy and effectiveness. These spreads can be as simple or as complicated as you wish, but don't make them too complex or you'll find them difficult to interpret and unwieldy to lay out. Having said that, there are no hard and fast rules about tarot spreads – the best tarot spread is the one that works best for you.

MOTIVES SPREAD

The questioner's current circumstances

The other person's current circumstances

The other person's current motives

The other person's current methods

The way forward

The questioner's choices

Outcome/ resolution

If you suspect that someone is finding ways of preventing you making the progress you think you deserve, or is deliberately obstructing you, you could create a spread that examines their motives and methods in detail.

SITUATIONS SPREAD

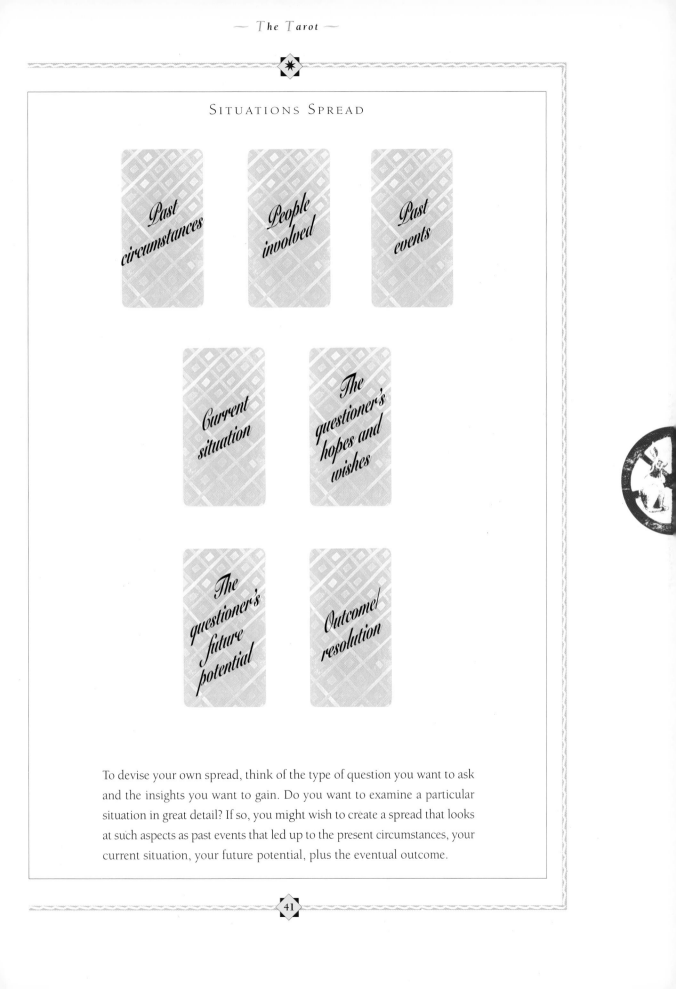

To devise your own spread, think of the type of question you want to ask and the insights you want to gain. Do you want to examine a particular situation in great detail? If so, you might wish to create a spread that looks at such aspects as past events that led up to the present circumstances, your current situation, your future potential, plus the eventual outcome.

THREE-CARD SPREADS

You can create a spread to answer any question you wish to ask or to tell you what the coming day or week will bring. All you need to do is decide on the shape of the spread, and what each card will represent, and then shuffle the cards and lay them out. If the spread doesn't work properly, perhaps because you need to incorporate other elements or the categories are in the wrong order, you can just start again.

A very simple home-made spread is the three-card spread, which can serve for many different situations. The cards can represent the past, present and future; if you want to know what the coming day will bring they can represent the morning, afternoon and evening; or if you want to know about your current circumstances, the cards could stand for your health, career and love life, or any other categories that you choose.

PAST, PRESENT AND FUTURE SPREAD

CURRENT CIRCUMSTANCES SPREAD

THE DAY AHEAD SPREAD

Morning

Afternoon

Evening

RELATIONSHIPS SPREAD

Friends

Family

Colleagues

POTENTIALS SPREAD

Talents

Creativity

Hidden Assets

DECISIONS SPREAD

first course of action

second course of action

If you're currently trying to reach an important decision and need help in making up your mind, you could devise a spread that shows you the possible ramifications of your actions. For instance, you could arrange two rows of three cards each, with the top one representing your feelings, the circumstances and the outcome of one course of action, and the bottom one repeating these categories for the other course of action.

A nineteenth-century illustration showing fortune-telling in the Bavarian Tyrol

The tarot is a very personal tool, so don't feel constrained by what you believe are the accepted ways of using it. If you find that cutting the cards four times brings you better results than cutting them three times, then that is what you should do. You may prefer to fan out the cards in front of you and choose them at random, rather than deal them off the top of the pack. Alternatively, you may devise other ways of selecting the cards. For instance, you might ask the questioner to choose a number. Let's say they opt for the number 14: you count down the pack until you reach the fourteenth card, after which you start dealing out the cards for the spread. Or you could deal out the cards, face down, until the questioner tells you to stop. You then deal out the spread from the remaining cards. You could even use a pendulum to select individual cards when they are fanned out in front of you. Experiment until you find what works for you, and ignore any books that tell you there's only one way to read the tarot properly, because that isn't true. The key to successful tarot reading is to find your own way of using and interpreting the cards, but always to treat them with respect. If you do this, you'll find the tarot very enjoyable and satisfying.

Cartomancy

The next time you take out a pack of cards ready to play a game with them, consider this – they were originally used for prophecy, and no one would have dreamed of using them for such frivolous purposes as entertainment and gambling. The earliest known cards were given the Hebrew name naibi, *which means 'to foretell', and they were treated with immense respect. Today, tarot cards are most often used for divination, and what we now call 'playing' cards are used for just that. Yet if you use them for their original purpose, to foretell the future, you'll be surprised at the accuracy of the messages they can give you. And if you are already familiar with the tarot, you will be intrigued by the similarities, as well as the differences, between tarot and playing cards.*

THERE ARE ALMOST as many theories about the exact origins of playing cards as there are interpretations of their meanings. Their history has been further clouded by periods when they were banned by Church or State – it was generally believed that cards were too good for the 'common people' and, besides, might lead them into all sorts of sinful practices. Yet, despite (or, perhaps because of) edicts like these, playing cards prospered and were soon used for games of chance as well as fortune-telling. By the nineteenth century, cartomancy (divination through cards) was wildly popular, with several noted exponents, including both the celebrated Madame Le Normand and also Monsieur Etteilla (who had reversed his real name, Alliette). Etteilla, an eighteenth-century Frenchman who was variously described as a wigmaker and/or Professor of Algebra, devised his own system of tarot cards. A huge success in Paris, he apparently foretold the deaths of several noblemen in the Revolution. Madame Le Normand, a celebrated tarot-reader and clairvoyant, was very popular in high society, and had several important clients, including the Empress Josephine. Incidentally, Josephine first learned of her dazzling future, involving marriage to Napoleon, followed by disgrace, from a cartomancer in the West Indies.

A French fortune-telling poster

CHOOSING A PACK OF CARDS

The beauty of cartomancy is that almost every household owns a pack of playing cards that can be pressed into service. Unlike the tarot, you don't have to buy a special pack although you may wish to do so, choosing one whose design and shape strongly appeal to you. If you're fortunate, you may even find a pack of playing cards that has been specially designed for cartomancy and is illustrated with symbols that will help your readings, just as some tarot packs contain illustrated Minor Arcana cards. Another bonus of using playing cards for divination is that they don't carry the same negative associations as tarot cards. While some people are wary or suspicious of the power of the tarot, they feel quite confident handling what they consider to be 'ordinary' playing cards. Yet, once you've used the cards to give readings, you'll realize that they aren't ordinary at all.

Incidentally, if you do decide to take up cartomancy, it is a good idea to use the pack of cards solely for predictive work and not to allow anyone to play snap or poker with it.

If you're a novice cartomancer, there may be another reason for you choosing playing cards instead of the tarot – there are fewer meanings to

These Austrian cards have suits of hearts, acorns, bells and leaves

remember. After all, there are 52 playing cards (excluding the jokers), whereas there are 78 tarot cards, which is quite a consideration when faced with the prospect of learning what each one means. The tarot pack is larger because it contains the 22 trump cards of the Major Arcana, as well as the 56 cards of the Minor Arcana from which our playing cards are believed to have originally descended.

Tarot cards have four court cards (King, Queen, Knight and Page) in each suit, whereas playing cards have three (King, Queen and Jack). The suits have different names although they share the same origins and virtually the same meanings. The tarot suit that corresponds to each playing card suit is shown on page 50.

There appear to be strong symbolic links between cartomancy and astrology, all based on numbers. To start with, there are 52 cards in a pack of playing cards, matching the number of weeks there are in the year.

In addition, there are four suits, matching the four astrological elements – Clubs correspond to the Fire element (Aries, Leo and Sagittarius); Diamonds to the Earth element (Taurus, Virgo and Capricorn); Spades to the Air element (Gemini, Libra and Aquarius); and Hearts to the Water element (Cancer, Scorpio and Pisces).

There are also 13 cards in each suit, just as there are 13 months in a lunar year (which is used in Chinese astrology). And, finally, there are 12 court cards, and 12 signs of the zodiac.

COMBINING THE TAROT AND PLAYING CARDS

If you wish to study both the tarot and cartomancy in depth, you'll discover that there are subtle differences in the interpretation of the Minor Arcana and its corresponding 'pip' playing cards. (A 'pip' card is one of the cards numbered 1–10 in a pack of playing cards.) However, these variations are so slight that it seems far more logical to keep the same interpretations for each system, with only the court cards having different meanings, especially if you are new to both systems of divination. Interpretations of all the Minor Arcana cards appear in the tarot chapter, and these can easily be used for their corresponding playing cards. Very brief interpretations of each card, which will act as memory-joggers, are given in this chapter.

If you're already familiar with the tarot, but would like to learn cartomancy, all you need do is mentally convert each playing card into its Minor Arcana equivalent, remembering the following rule:

HEARTS are CUPS

DIAMONDS are PENTACLES

CLUBS are WANDS

SPADES are SWORDS

The Queen of Diamonds

THE SYMBOLISM OF THE COURT CARDS

As with the tarot, the court cards represent people known to the questioner (the term for the person for whom you are reading the cards). In the tarot, all the court cards can signify situations or desirable states of mind instead of actual people. But in cartomancy, there is less interpretative scope. Kings represent men, and Queens symbolize women, but Jacks are more open to interpretation. They may represent a child or adolescent of either sex, especially when accompanied in a spread by a King or Queen, or they could symbolize a partner in love or work who's younger than the questioner. If they appear in a spread with the King or Queen of the same suit, they may signify the thoughts of that person, in which case these will take on the colouring of the cards around them – loving thoughts if surrounded by Hearts, sinister or malicious ones if surrounded by Spades, and so on.

CHOOSING A SIGNIFICATOR

Some readings require the card-reader to select a card, known as a significator, which represents the questioner. Naturally, men choose Kings, women choose Queens and young people choose Jacks. But which suit do you use? There are several systems available – you can select the suit according to the type of career it represents, the traditional colouring of the face and hair, the emotional and mental attitude that it symbolizes or the astrological element to which it corresponds.

With such a wide choice open to you, you'll be extremely fortunate if you can find a suit that fulfils all these requirements. Let's say you're looking for the significator of a female questioner who was born under the Air sign of Gemini, is elderly, white-haired, luxury-loving and used to be an estate agent. Do you choose the Queen of Spades (Air element), the Queen of Hearts (white hair), the Queen of Clubs (luxury) or the Queen of Diamonds (career in property)? Or do you forget the whole thing in sheer frustration? No, you don't. Choose one category that makes the most sense to you, and stick with it. If you're very interested in astrology, you may wish to use the relevant astrological element when choosing a significator. If you are fascinated by people's personalities, use these as your guide. As you become a more proficient cartomancer, you'll become more confident about the meaning of each court card and the person it represents, and you may adjust your guidelines accordingly.

What you should never do is flit between one set of guidelines and another within the same reading, according to which one is most favourable (even though this is tempting, especially when reading your own cards). Don't decide that the King of Diamonds represents your Capricorn questioner, only to change tack halfway through and decide that the Queen of Clubs symbolizes a dark-haired woman.

Some books suggest removing the significator from the pack and putting it to one side before you give a reading, but it seems much more logical to choose your significator and then see if it appears in the reading. If it does, note its

CHOOSING THE SUIT

Suit	Traditional Colouring	Personality Type	Astrological Element	Careers
♥	Blond or white hair Blue or green eyes Fair complexion	Warm, friendly, affectionate, loving, creative	WATER (Cancer, Scorpio, Pisces)	Caring professions, creative and artistic professions, education
♣	Brown hair Brown or hazel eyes Ruddy complexion	Energetic, lively, luxury-loving	FIRE (Aries, Leo, Sagittarius)	Media, travel, business
♦	Mousy or red hair Green eyes Freckles, fair complexion	Confident, practical, materialistic	EARTH (Taurus, Virgo, Capricorn)	Banking, real estate
♠	Dark brown or black hair Brown or black eyes Dark complexion	Powerful, intelligent, melancholy	AIR (Gemini, Libra, Aquarius)	Law, big business, traditionally all professions connected with death

position carefully. If it appears in the centre of the spread, the questioner is in the middle of an important situation. If it's to one side, the situation is either just beginning or just ending.

LIKES ATTRACT, OPPOSITES REPEL

The suits of the court cards that appear in a reading will also tell you about the affinities involved. Court cards of the same suit indicate a close relationship, so if, for example, the King of Spades appears in a reading for a questioner whose significator is the Queen of Spades, you can assume that he represents her husband or whichever man is most important to her. (However, this rule varies according to the nature of the reading. So, if the reading concerns her career, this man is probably a friendly colleague or boss rather than her husband.) The Jack of Spades could represent the questioner's child, a friend or her thoughts.

You must also bear in mind that each suit has an opposite number, indicating a negative affinity. Hearts are opposed to Diamonds, and Clubs are opposed to Spades. So, if the King of Clubs appears in a reading for a woman symbolized by the Queen of Spades, you know that he'll bring tension or difficulty – perhaps they're having a love affair that isn't going well, or he's a jealous colleague. If the King of Hearts or Diamonds turns up, you interpret him in the usual way.

A fortune-teller at a French fair

HEARTS

As its name suggests, this suit rules emotional matters, such as love affairs, relationships, friendships and feelings of affection. Hearts also rule creativity, fertility and abundance. In addition, they're connected with possessions, the home and educational matters. Hearts have an uplifting effect on their surrounding cards; when several appear in a spread they indicate that the questioner will experience love and happiness, even if the other cards show that there will also be problems along the way.

DIAMONDS

Diamonds rule all material matters, including money, property and status, plus whatever matters most to the questioner. As might be imagined, such topics can provoke angry outbursts so life is often very colourful when several Diamonds appear in a reading. They also represent vitality and energy, but they're affected by the cards around them so their natural exuberance will be tempered if they're surrounded by Spades.

CLUBS

Words, negotiations and business matters are ruled by Clubs. They're also connected with energy, enterprise, progress, ambition and personal growth. Clubs can indicate imminent travel, especially if it's connected with the questioner's career or ambitions, as well as clubs, organizations and societies.

An illustration from a nineteenth-century French satire on cartomancy

SPADES

If Hearts are considered to be the most favourable suit, Spades are definitely the least fortunate, since they indicate problems, possible arguments, disputes, worries, delays and losses. Yet they take on the colouring of the cards around them, so a Spade surrounded by Hearts and Clubs will lose a lot of its sting (although the miserable Ten of Spades will remain unchanged). Ideas and swift action are also connected with Spades.

THE PIP CARDS

Interpretations of these cards are given in the Minor Arcana section in the tarot chapter (see pages 21–32), but the brief descriptions given here will jog your memory and fire your intuition when you use this chapter.

 A new relationship or a fresh start in an existing one. A new creative phase.

 Money is on the way. A venture that means a lot to the questioner. A ring.

The questioner should take the initiative and grasp opportunities. The birth of a wonderful idea.

A new project or relationship that will really engross the questioner.

A new partnership or the signing of an agreement – a marriage licence?

 The questioner needs to juggle either their finances or their time.

 The questioner knows they're in a strong position and should act accordingly.

 The questioner must break free of their current stalemate.

 A joyful celebration or the happy outcome of an existing problem.

 Hard work will bring financial and personal rewards and satisfaction.

 An excellent time to communicate ideas and make decisions.

 Heartbreak or illness, but out of bad will come good.

 A dreary routine that can be broken if an opportunity is seized.

 Emotional or financial security but potential greed or complacency.

 Success and achievement after a period of hard work.

 The questioner should take a breather after recent efforts.

 Regret, sadness, loss or disappointment, often in a relationship.

 Something that the questioner values will be put in jeopardy.

Nothing will go according to plan. Things should not be left to chance.

 The questioner can turn their talents into money and a career.

 The questioner should cut their losses in some way.

 Life will be busy, with travel or a lot of work on the way.

 Misplaced nostalgia or an element from the past will affect the future.

 Although circumstances appear bleak, there is a way forward.

 Good financial news or generosity towards loved ones.

 A cherished dream or wish will come true. The start of a sexy relationship?

 Recent efforts will reach a successful conclusion and reap rewards.

 Material security and emotional satisfaction are on the way.

 A move away from a stressful situation to more harmonious circumstances.

 The questioner should conserve their energies and their finances.

 Wonderful opportunities, enormous potential and tremendous creativity.

 The questioner must acknowledge and surmount severe worries and anxieties.

 The questioner feels justifiably proud but shouldn't rest on their laurels.

 Emotional fulfilment, completion and lasting happiness.

 Willpower, courage and determination will win the day.

 The completion of something that will bring abundance, joy and money.

 The questioner must escape from an unpleasant situation.

 The questioner is shouldering a heavy burden that may be self-imposed.

 The end of a relationship will lead to a new beginning.

 The culmination of an unpleasant situation, leading to new beginnings.

THE COURT CARDS

Remember that Hearts and Diamonds are opposites, as are Clubs and Spades.

Jack of Hearts

Traditionally, this card is said to represent Cupid or Eros, so it's a wonderful card to appear in a spread because it suggests that love could be on the way – if so, this will be supported by other cards, such as the Ace or Ten of Hearts. Take note of the cards that surround this Jack because the person it signifies may not always be trustworthy – watch out for Spades, which suggest mischief or someone playing games. The Jack of Hearts can symbolize the questioner's dearest friend or their lover. Alternatively, he may represent loving thoughts that are being directed towards the questioner. If the Jack of Hearts represents a person, it's someone who's flirtatious, lively and attractive. They may belong to one of the Water signs – Cancer, Scorpio and Pisces.

Jack of Diamonds

Life can be very busy when this card appears, because it signifies movement, travel and the arrival of news. For instance, the questioner may soon hear something of importance, especially if it concerns their business interests or money matters. Alternatively, the Jack of Diamonds may indicate a busy social time ahead, with unexpected or exciting invitations. If it appears with the King or Queen of Diamonds, this card represents that person's thoughts – these will be coloured by their surrounding cards. If

the Jack of Diamonds represents a person, it's someone who's lively, positive, entertaining and energetic. They may belong to one of the Earth signs – Taurus, Virgo or Capricorn.

Jack of Clubs

This card represents friendship, so can signify a close friend of the questioner or someone who will lend them plenty of support, whether emotional, physical or financial. The Jack of Clubs is also linked with ideas and conversations, so can symbolize anything from an important discussion to a comforting chat. If he represents a person in the questioner's life, it's someone of either sex who is affectionate, friendly and practical. They may belong to one of the Fire signs – Aries, Leo and Sagittarius. If the card appears with the King or Queen of Clubs, it represents that person's thoughts.

Jack of Spades

The questioner should take care when the Jack of Spades appears in a reading, because it can signify someone of either sex who isn't to be relied upon. They may speak with a forked tongue, deliberately misleading the questioner, or they may inadvertently give them the wrong information. This person may also be rather devious and is certainly not to be trusted – if the questioner is currently involved in an important business or financial arrangement they should be very choosy about whom they deal with. They should also take care not to divulge any secrets to someone who could use them as a weapon or whose gossip will cause trouble. Sometimes, the Jack of Spades simply represents the thoughts of the King or Queen of Spades.

Queen of Hearts

This woman is emotional, loving (perhaps passionate), intuitive and friendly. She's sensitive, faithful and trustworthy, and puts a lot of effort into her relationships, which mean a great deal to her. People are instinctively drawn to her, attracted by her innate charm and affectionate temperament. She may also be creative, and enjoys using her prolific artistic talents. Her home and family are important to her, and may act as a refuge. At times, she needs to be alone with her thoughts, in order to recharge her emotional batteries. Sometimes, the Queen of Hearts can represent an important loving relationship, regardless of the sex of the person involved. She may symbolize someone born under one of the Water signs – Cancer, Scorpio or Pisces.

Queen of Diamonds

This is a popular lady, because she's enthusiastic, entertaining and attractive. She has plenty of friends and admirers, and is playfully flirtatious. However, she doesn't take such relationships seriously because she's loyal to the man in her life. Although lively and fun-loving on the surface, this woman keeps her emotions to herself

and can be reluctant to show how she really feels. Her powers of intuition can be strong, and she enjoys using them. She may have a materialistic streak, or will enjoy being able to afford the good things in life. She may belong to one of the Earth signs – Taurus, Virgo or Capricorn.

Queen of Clubs

This lady takes a very practical approach to life. She's down-to-earth, well-organized and reliable. Her sensuous, affectionate and generous personality wins her many friends. She's intelligent and enjoys serious conversations in which she can air her views. Money means a lot to her and she makes sure that she always has a little cash to fall back on in case of a rainy day. She enjoys a relatively high standard of living, and will do her best to find a partner who has the same outlook on life. This woman may belong to one of the Fire signs – Aries, Leo or Sagittarius.

Queen of Spades

Traditionally, this card represents a woman who lives on her own, possibly as a result of divorce or widowhood, and who has experienced many hardships in her life. She's very intelligent and often has a good career in one of the professions, because she's ambitious and knows what she wants to achieve. Some sources say the Queen of Spades can be sly, devious and cunning. It may be difficult to grow close to this woman because her innate reserve and apparently cool emotions set her apart from those around her. However, her feelings may run very deep,

although she doesn't like people knowing this. The woman symbolized by this card may have been born under one of the three Air signs – Gemini, Libra or Aquarius.

King of Hearts

This man is kind-hearted, affectionate and generous. He may also be artistic and, possibly, psychic. As his name suggests, the King of Hearts is the classic lover – handsome, sexually attractive, romantic, sensuous and charismatic. He takes a lot of effort with his appearance and succeeds in looking very striking. Most of us would be delighted to have him turn up in a reading. However, this pleasant, popular persona can mask a shy, retiring man who is prone to moodiness and petulant silences. He certainly needs to spend time by himself every now and then, and his partner must understand this. He may symbolize a man born under one of the Water signs – Cancer, Scorpio or Pisces.

King of Diamonds

You can't mistake this man, because he's usually the life and soul of the party. He's the raconteur, the man with a smile and a joke for everyone, and he enjoys being the centre of attention. His confidence, self-assurance and sense of humour ensure his popularity, but underlying such characteristics is a strong need to succeed in life, both emotionally and materially. His ambitions are very important to him, and he expends a great deal of energy in achieving his aims, possibly even at the cost of personal relationships.

He may represent a man who belongs to one of the Earth signs – Taurus, Virgo or Capricorn.

King of Clubs

One of the most striking traits of the King of Clubs is his practical approach to the world. If you're in trouble, this is probably the first man you will turn to, either because he can help you in a professional capacity or simply because he's a sympathetic friend. He's a man who enjoys the best that life can offer, and he's prepared to work hard in order to be able to afford such things. He's a prudent saver, who is keen on making financial provision for his future and that of his family. The King of Clubs may represent a man who belongs to one of the Fire signs – Aries, Leo or Sagittarius.

King of Spades

Here is a powerful man, probably successful in his career and in an influential position – possible professions include medicine, law and politics. He enjoys his autonomy, since he has a strong need for power, although he's unlikely ever to let it get out of hand. He's probably well-respected by the people who know him, although they may not warm to him – he's too aloof and businesslike for that. He's a faithful and honest lover, yet he may not be a very imaginative one, and he could be prone to jealousy or possessiveness because of his strong need to exercise control over others. The King of Swords may represent a man born under one of the three Air signs – Gemini, Libra or Aquarius.

INTERPRETING THE CARDS

Playing cards are laid out in spreads, in the same way as tarot cards (see page 32), but the balance of cards can be as important as the cards themselves. For instance, if Diamonds are surrounded by many cards of a different suit, they are said to reflect the meaning of this suit. Hearts can enliven an otherwise dreary reading, while many Spades cast a pall over the other cards. Clubs add a sense of movement and urgency.

Cartomancy books often go into great detail about the combination of cards that appear in a reading, such as four Aces or three Queens. Although this means there's more to learn and remember, these combinations give the reading extra layers of meaning. (You might also like to use them when reading the tarot, to see if they have the same effects.) Here is a selection of combinations; the figures refer to the number of Aces, Kings, etc.

Aces

2 Big changes are on the way.

3 Good news; a fortunate opportunity.

4 Tremendous success.

Kings

2 Convivial company or a new business partner.

3 Success in business.

4 Tremendous good fortune. Recognition, success, acclaim.

Queens

2 Encouragement from a friend.

3 A busy social time. Beware of spreading gossip as it could backfire.

4 The threat of scandal and treachery, possibly through women

Jacks

2 Guard against deceit or trickery. Watch what you say.

3 Hard to get new projects off the ground. People may bicker.

4 Major quarrels, deep divisions in personal or business relationships.

Tens

2 Changes in the environment.

3 Monetary problems. Possible litigation.

4 A project will reach a very successful and satisfying conclusion.

Nines

2 Small gains in either the career or in personal relationships.

3 Success is just around the corner.

4 A happy surprise will soon arrive. There will also be financial benefits.

Eights

2 A possible journey, although it will not be abroad.

3 Domestic problems.

4 It will be very difficult to escape from a tricky situation.

Sevens

2 Fun and entertainment.

3 Pregnancy, or alternatively the birth of an enjoyable enterprise.

4 Conspiracies or secret enemies. Proceed with great caution.

Two ladies learn their fate through the cards

SPECIFIC COMBINATIONS

Ace of Hearts and Ace of Diamonds signify an important love affair or wedding.

Ace and Ten of Diamonds mean overseas news.

Ace of Diamonds and Ten of Hearts signify a big romance, possibly leading to marriage.

Ace of Clubs and Nine of Spades indicate that someone will let the questioner down badly.

Ace and Eight of Spades signal disappointments.

A King or Queen followed by a Heart indicates someone who wishes to become the questioner's friend or lover.

A King or Queen surrounded by Diamonds denotes a rich person.

Several court cards together indicate a sociable, convivial time.

A court card between two pip cards of equal numerical value shows that the person represented will experience difficulties.

Ten of Hearts and Ten of Diamonds suggest a lovely financial surprise.

Nine of Hearts and Nine of Diamonds mean that a wish will come true.

Nine of Swords and Nine of Clubs signify a very unhappy time.

Eight of Clubs and any Diamond indicate the arrival of a letter bearing financial news.

Eight and Five of Spades indicate a false friend.

Seven of Diamonds and Ten of Swords mean trouble over money.

Seven of Hearts and Seven of Diamonds signify a new love.

THE FOUR ACES SPREAD

This is a very simple but effective spread that's invaluable for answering one of the questions that's most commonly asked in cartomancy – 'Will my wish come true?' You can, of course, give the questioner a complex reading involving several cards, but this spread gives a simple 'yes' or 'no' response that can act as a starting point for a fuller reading using a more complicated spread.

First, you should remove all the Twos, Threes, Fours, Fives and Sixes from the pack, to create a smaller deck of 32 cards. This is the number of cards that has been traditionally used in cartomancy. Put the discarded cards to one side and hand the deck of 32 cards to the questioner. Ask them to shuffle well while thinking of their question, then hand the cards back to you.

Deal the first 13 cards off the top of the pack and place them face up on the table. If any of the four Aces have appeared, remove them and place them, face up, by themselves in the order in which they appeared. This is extremely important because it will tell you when and if the wish will come true. In the unlikely event that all four Aces have turned up, you are now ready to interpret them. If not, you must deal out the cards

again. To do this, gather up the remainder of the discarded 13 cards, place them on top of the rest of the pack, and ask the questioner to shuffle them again, then hand them back to you. Deal out another 13 cards and look for the Aces. If you find any, put them with the other Aces in the order in which they appeared. You can repeat this for a third and final time, if necessary. Usually, the questioner finds this process intriguing.

The earlier the four Aces appear, the more likely the wish is to come true. If they all materialize in the first deal, the questioner can be sure of success. If the Aces are completed in the second deal, the questioner is guaranteed good luck. If the third deal still hasn't produced all the Aces, the questioner's wish is not so likely to be granted or there will be considerable delays.

Which Ace appeared first? If it's the Ace of Spades, the questioner will need to exert an enormous amount of effort to have their wish come true. If it's the Ace of Clubs, they'll need to rely on someone's goodwill. If it's the Ace of Diamonds, they'll have to spend money in order for their wish to come about. If it's the Ace of Hearts, success will come easily.

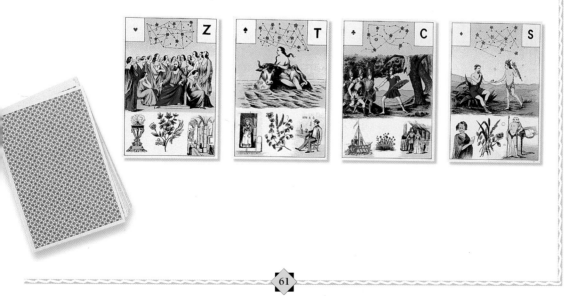

THE WEEK AHEAD SPREAD

This is an excellent spread for determining the general flavour of the week ahead, although it has to be said that it's unlikely to give a chronological timetable of events. Unfortunately, the cards aren't often that obliging. Nevertheless, this spread is a good indicator of the way the week's energies will flow, and will warn the questioner of any potential pitfalls. You'll also gain an overview of the week from the colours and nature of the cards involved – a predominance of red cards, for example, indicates a happy, enjoyable week; mostly Clubs means that business matters will go very well; mostly Spades signifies disappointments and delays; several court cards point to plenty of social events.

This spread is excellent practice if you're learning to read the cards, because it teaches you to read cards in pairs and, therefore, to make up a story that links them. Sometimes the link will be obvious and easy to interpret, such as the King and Queen of Hearts that appear in the sample spread. They indicate a time of great affection and love. At other times you may have to think hard to come up with a suitable interpretation for what seem to be a mismatched pair of cards. Let your intuition and your imagination guide you.

Before you begin, choose a significator for the questioner. In this case, it was the Queen of Wands, based on the questioner's Sun sign. Some cartomancers recommend placing the significator in the centre of the spread, but this prevents the chance of it appearing somewhere in the reading, which can be very revealing.

Use the full deck of 52 cards. Ask the questioner to shuffle them well, then to cut them into two piles. Take the second pile and deal out seven cards off the top, placing the first one on the far left and arranging them in a semi-circle. The seventh card will be on the far right.

Now hand all the remaining cards back to the questioner and ask them to shuffle them again, then cut them once more. Take the second pile and deal out the top seven cards, laying them on top of the first set of cards.

INTERPRETATION OF EXAMPLE

Jack of Clubs/Ace of Spades

The questioner will have an intriguing conversation which will spark off an entirely new and engrossing interest.

Eight of Spades/Ace of Diamonds

If the questioner can conquer a particular fear, it will lead on to a wonderful new·beginning.

Six of Clubs/Eight of Clubs

A journey connected with a business venture will be a great success.

Six of Hearts/Queen of Clubs

Here's the significator. She'll enjoy being surrounded by her family.

King of Hearts/Queen of Hearts

Love! A romantic or affectionate interlude is on the way.

Two of Spades/Eight of Hearts

The questioner will have to walk away from something that means a lot to them in order to resolve a stalemate.

Seven of Diamonds/Five of Hearts

Something will be a source of tremendous regret, yet the questioner should look to the future and fresh opportunities.

The cards that were chosen show it will be a good week, but not without its difficult moments, indicated by two tense combinations – the Two of Spades with the Eight of Hearts, and the Seven of Diamonds with the Five of Hearts. There is an equal number of red and black cards, indicating a balance between positive and negative experiences for the questioner, with more Hearts than any other suit, thus giving an enjoyable, sociable and loving flavour to the week.

CHIEN DE PIQUE

This method is French, and focuses on four areas of the questioner's life, with particular emphasis on their fate, as symbolized by the Jack of Spades.

Chien de Pique uses the complete deck of cards. Give the questioner the deck and ask them to shuffle well, then to hand it back to you. Now go through the pack, looking for four cards. These are the Jack of Spades, which represents the questioner's fate; the questioner's significator (the King or Queen of the suit that represents them most accurately); the Seven of the same suit, for the questioner's thoughts; and the Ace of Hearts, for love and their home life.

Go through the pack, turning up two cards at a time. Whenever you turn over one of the chosen four cards, put that card, plus its partner, face up on the table. Arrange the cards in the order they appear in. When you've gone through the deck you'll probably have eight cards in total, arranged in four rows of two cards each. If you turn up two of the chosen cards at the same time, then you'll have six cards in total by the time you've gone through the pack. Now spread out the discarded cards in a fan and ask the questioner to choose eight. Place the first card chosen to the left of the top row of cards, the second to the right of the top row, the third to the left of the second row, and so on, until sixteen cards are laid out (it'll be twelve if two of the chosen cards appeared as a pair).

You're now ready to interpret the cards in the usual way. The other cards in the same row as the significator indicate the circumstances around the questioner at the time of the reading; those in the same row as the Ace of Hearts describe the state of their emotions and their home life; those in the same row as the Seven indicate the questioner's thoughts, and those in the same row as the Jack of Spades describe the questioner's destiny or fate.

In the spread shown here, the significator chosen was the Queen of Clubs, and so the Seven of Clubs was also used. The questioner had just been offered a wonderful career opportunity which she was excited about but she was worried about the amount of work it would entail. At the time of the reading she was single and hoping that a new man would soon enter her life.

CATEGORIES AND INTERPRETATION

Top row – the questioner's circumstances

The Queen of Diamonds indicates that a fair-haired woman will be of great help to the questioner, especially where her work (Three of Diamonds) is concerned. The Six of Hearts suggests this work will come from her reputation.

Second row – the questioner's fate

A meeting or some form of communication (Three of Clubs) with a friendly person (Jack of Hearts) will bring the prospect of tremendous material success (Nine of Diamonds). This adds weight to the previous interpretation.

Third row – the questioner's emotions and family

Love is definitely in the air! The questioner will soon enjoy a sensuous relationship (Nine of Hearts) with a loving man (King of Hearts). She'll enjoy tremendous satisfaction, both materially and emotionally (Ten of Diamonds).

Fourth row – the questioner's thoughts

These echo the career prospects theme. She's preoccupied with the opportunities that have been offered her (Seven of Hearts) and knows that she's able to rise to the challenge (Two of Clubs), but mustn't burn herself out (Four of Spades).

Sun Sign Astrology

'What Sun sign are you?' It's a question we've all been asked at one time or another and, curiously enough, even the people who profess to dislike astrology will always be able to answer. Sun sign astrology, which focuses on the zodiac sign occupied by the Sun at the time of birth, is only one facet of a much broader and deeper study. Even so, knowing someone's birth sign provides an insight into their character and will help you to gain a general understanding of the way they tick. It gives an excellent glimpse into your own personality too. Knowing someone's Sun sign will also help you to appreciate the dynamics of your relationship, and so this chapter includes compatibility charts between the signs in love and business.

ARIES

21 March – 20 April

RULED BY MARS

BELONGS TO THE FIRE ELEMENT

COLOUR IS FIERY RED

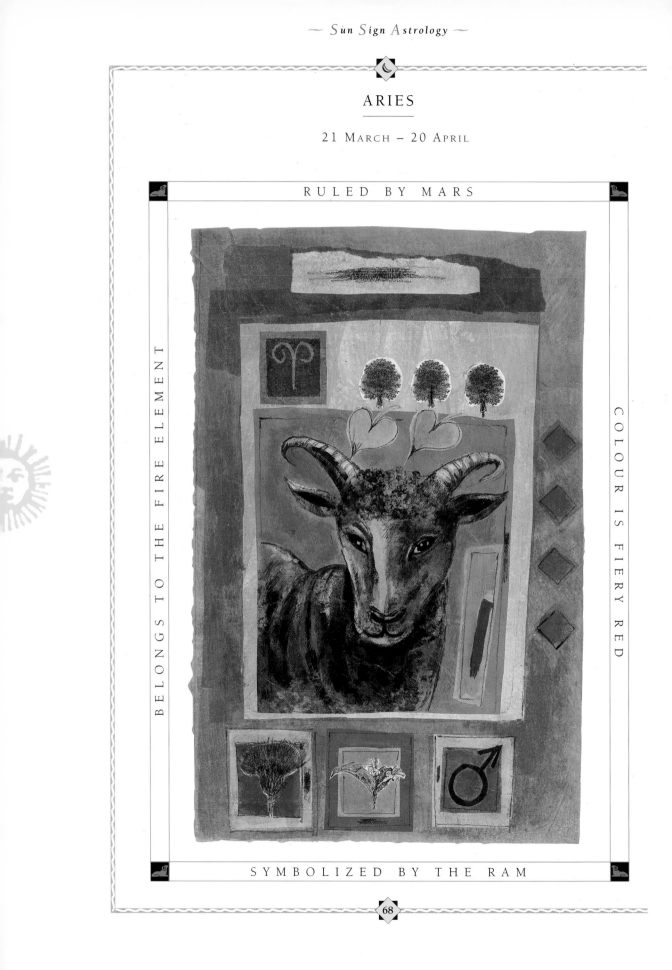

SYMBOLIZED BY THE RAM

NICE GUYS FINISH LAST, but Arians have to come first. That has nothing to do with how nice they are, but is all about their position in the zodiac. Aries is the first sign, and the day that the Sun enters Aries marks the first day of spring in the northern hemisphere. This means that Arians are psychologically programmed to be at the head of any queue. Their first thought is to put their own considerations above those of other people, even if their second thought reverses this. Yet this does not make Arians deliberately selfish, although the sign certainly has its fair share of self-centred mortals. Rather, they react in the way that a child does, thinking 'Me first!'

Arians are born with a sense of adventure, and many Arian babies arrive either early or very rapidly, as if they're in a hurry to get out of the womb and into the world. This sense of urgency never leaves them – they're always eager for new experiences and they retain a childlike enthusiasm throughout their lives. However, although this impetuous, inquisitive nature means they have lots of adventures, it can sometimes lead Arians into areas that other signs instinctively avoid. Arians rush in headfirst, sometimes with

marvellous results and other times with disastrous ones. Not that Arians care. Well, not at the time, anyway. They're far too swept up in their new venture to pay attention to such mundane considerations as whether it's wise to buy that house without having it surveyed or what will happen to their job while they're driving across America in a pink 1954 Cadillac. It's only later on, when things haven't worked out in quite the way they expected, that the Arian will feel disappointed, not to say completely and utterly disillusioned. They may then ask you, in what sounds suspiciously like an accusation, why you did not warn them. At this point it's best to change the subject – your protestations will be met with a puzzled silence or vehement denials. Either way, you won't get anywhere so you might as well save your breath. If you want a row, you've chosen the right person, as Arians are extremely hot-tempered, although their anger subsides as quickly as it flares up. In the meantime, you may be tempted to take cover in case a few missiles are hurled in your direction.

It's this childlike enthusiasm for life, so typical of their Fire element, that makes Arians such delightful company, and they're usually enviably popular. They have big hearts which are often broken, because Arians tend to put people on pedestals. Their loving, kind and trusting personalities mean they always look for the best in other people and turn a blind eye to any characteristics they don't like, but this attitude causes a lot of heartache if the person concerned lets the Arian down. They simply can't understand what went wrong.

Arians are very inventive and can come up with some wonderfully inspired ideas, especially at work. The thought of having to see these plans through from start to finish, however, can fill them with horror, so they often prefer to get someone else to do the donkey work. Something else they can't abide is being followers rather than leaders. Arians have to be in charge and, although this can stray into imperiousness, it's usually expressed with grace and consideration.

TAURUS

21 April – 21 May

RULED BY VENUS

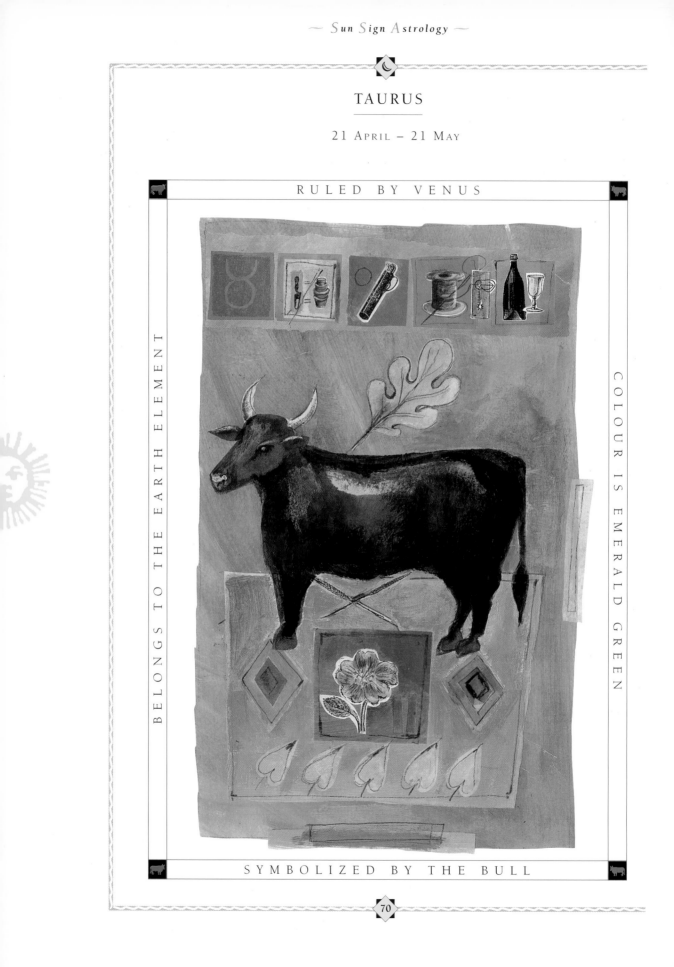

BELONGS TO THE EARTH ELEMENT

COLOUR IS EMERALD GREEN

SYMBOLIZED BY THE BULL

WHAT EXACTLY is a red rag to a bull? For Taureans, who are born under the sign of the Bull, it's anything connected with change. Of course, most Taureans will deny this hotly, saying how unfair it is that they've been landed with this stuck-in-a-rut tag, and that it simply isn't true. But once you've talked to a Taurean for long, you'll gain a very strong impression of their need for stability. They like a sense of continuity to flow through their lives, and what some signs might find predictable is simply comforting familiarity to Taureans.

One thing that Taureans find particularly difficult to accept is change for its own sake. This means that they can get very bogged down in routine and, even if this becomes so stultifying that they're climbing the walls, they may find it hard to break out of their rut. It can also be nearly impossible to persuade a Taurean to change their mind, even if there's an extremely good reason for them to do so. The more you argue your corner, the more they'll dig in their heels and doggedly stand their ground. This isn't to be awkward, in an Aquarian you-may-say-that's-white-but-I'm-calling-it-black way, but simply because they've made up their minds and they aren't going to budge. They are very strong-minded and this can turn into a stubborn and pig-headed streak.

Their desire for stability affects every area of a Taurean's life. They have a deep-rooted need for material security, so will work hard to ensure that they have somewhere comfortable to live. Their home means a great deal to them, not only as a haven but also as an outward symbol of their success in life. Something else that's vital to a Taurean's happiness is emotional security. Taureans need someone to love, and they are faithful, loyal and devoted partners. You don't have to play games or pretend to be hard to get, you simply have to prove that you're worthy of a Taurean's love and won't break their heart. You know where you are with a Taurean. Unfortunately, they also like to know where you are – literally. Taureans are notoriously possessive. They think they own you, just as they own their armchair or television, and if you don't like this you will have to nip it gently in the bud.

Taurus is ruled by Venus, the planet of love and luxury, which means that Taureans are no slouches when it comes to having a good time. They thoroughly enjoy eating and drinking, even if this is at the expense of a waistline as they get older – chocolate is one of their biggest temptations. This is the most sybaritic, sensuous and hedonistic of all the signs, and Taureans can be extremely voluptuous and sexy when they're with the right person. Most Taureans have a deep affinity with music and many have beautiful singing or speaking voices. Traditionally, they're the most physically attractive of the signs – news which may put many Leos' and Librans' noses firmly out of joint.

Nature is very important to Taureans. Even the most urban Taurean flourishes in the countryside, and many Taureans are excellent gardeners. Digging the soil helps them to diffuse any pent-up stress which would otherwise materialize in the form of illness (especially throat infections) or brooding. Taureans are easygoing and it takes a lot to make them lose their tempers, but once they do there'll be no mistaking their anger. It's far better to avoid arousing it in the first place.

GEMINI

22 May – 21 June

SOME SUN SIGNS are difficult to identify, but not Geminis. Look at their eyes – these are usually bright and restless. Geminis are fascinated by whatever is going on around them, because they love movement and action. They also retain an air of youthfulness, even in old age.

Very often, you will hear a Gemini before you see them. It might be their radio or CD that's playing, or they might be expounding their latest theory or chatting on a mobile phone. Geminis tend to be skilled communicators (they are ruled by  Mercury, the planet of communications) and enjoy staying in touch with friends by phone, letter, fax, e-mail, Internet, homing pigeon … you name it, a Gemini will try it. Their childlike enthusiasm for life means they're fascinated by gadgets, especially if these are small enough to fit into a pocket or bag. Electronic organizers are perfect toys for them.

One of the great astrological myths is that Geminis are schizophrenic, but this isn't true. Yes, they are extremely moody, and are usually either dancing on the ceiling or plunged into the depths of despond. But whereas schizophrenics switch from one personality to another, Geminis can be several people at the same time. The bright, bubbly Gemini may be chattering away but inside they could be feeling wretched.

Perhaps it's for these reasons that Geminis are often accused of being superficial. Some of them can certainly be emotionally flighty and reluctant to commit themselves to anyone for long, but for most of them it's more that they're always falling in love with new ideas, new people and new places, and then moving on to the next interest. Because they were born under the sign of the Twins, Geminis spend their whole lives searching for their soulmates. They never realize that the person they're looking for is inside them.

Geminis belong to the Air element, making them intelligent and primarily concerned with ideas. They are uncomfortable when discussing their feelings and may even try to fool themselves over some of their emotions, especially if these are very strong or painful. They enjoy sex but like to keep everything on a light, chatty level – intense, passionate encounters frighten them, although they'll enjoy recounting all the gory details to their friends.

They are extremely versatile and adaptable, so are suited to many occupations. However, they need to keep on the move as much as possible, and are par-  ticularly gifted sales people, journalists and writers. Unlike most Sun signs, Geminis can actually become ill when life grows too mundane or pre- dictable – they need the mental stimulation of being busy. Geminis live on their nerves, which keeps them slim but can exhaust them, make them irritable and leave them prone to insomnia. Their lungs, arms and hands are the vulnerable parts of the Gemini body – not helped by their tendency to gesticulate generously whenever they talk, regardless of whether anything is in the way.

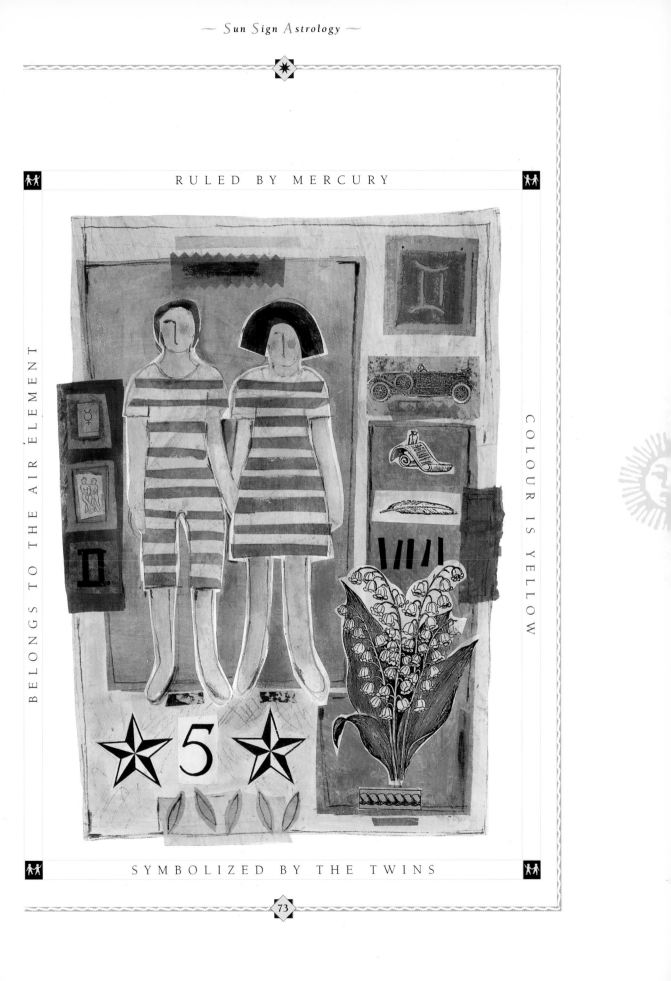

RULED BY MERCURY

BELONGS TO THE AIR ELEMENT

COLOUR IS YELLOW

SYMBOLIZED BY THE TWINS

CANCER

22 June – 22 July

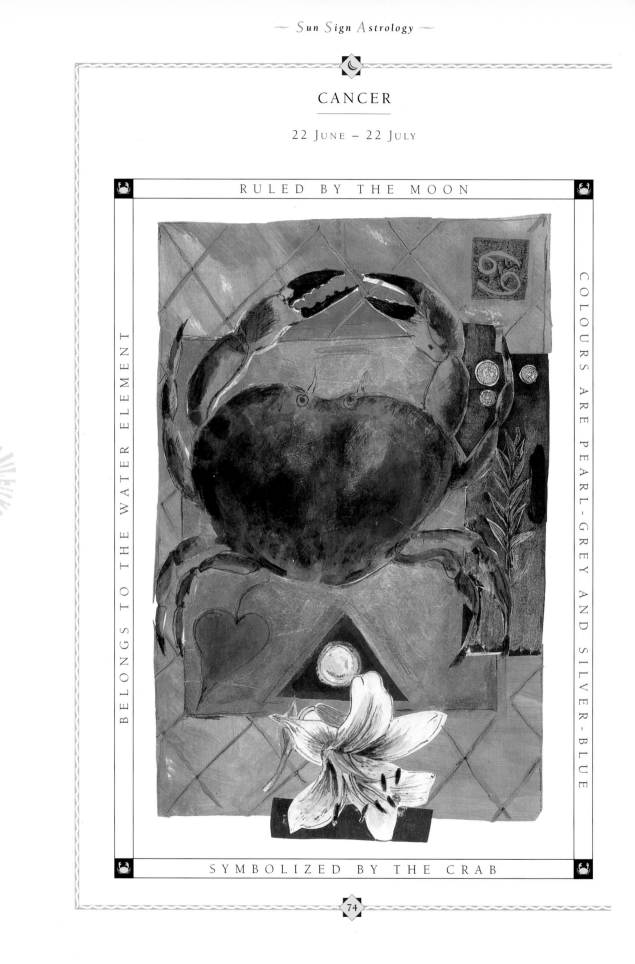

RULED BY THE MOON

BELONGS TO THE WATER ELEMENT

COLOURS ARE PEARL-GREY AND SILVER-BLUE

SYMBOLIZED BY THE CRAB

I F YOU WANT TO BE looked after, head straight for the nearest Cancerian. Their loving, sympathetic, tender and protective qualities will offer everything you need, especially if you also happen to enjoy home-cooking and creature comforts. Even Cancerians who don't know one end of a saucepan from the other are very caring, kind-hearted and affectionate.

Family matters are important for all Cancerians, whether they love their nearest and dearest or won't have anything to do with them. Either way, the family assumes great significance in a Cancerian's life. Most Cancerians who don't have

a family of their own create a ready-made version from close friends and associates. They may have a job that involves looking after other people's interests, in one of the caring professions or in the service industries, or they may simply amass a large, extended family.

Home is the great refuge for Cancerians. Like the crab which symbolizes this sign, Cancerians derive enormous comfort from retreating to their homes and shutting the front door on the rest of the world. Although some Cancerians will happily invite everyone round to their place, others prefer to keep their homes separate from the other areas of their life. If you know a Cancerian like this, you should consider it a great honour if you're ever ushered through their front door.

A typical Cancerian home is very cosy and comfortable. Cancerians enjoy being surrounded by mementoes, so will probably display many photographs and keepsakes that remind them of the past. There may also be quite a lot of clutter, because Cancerians are tremendous hoarders and find it virtually impossible to throw anything away. The minimal look is anathema to them.

This same tenacity and reluctance to let go of the past can spill over into their relationships. Even when it's obvious to everyone else that a Cancerian is clinging on to a partnership that's all over bar the shouting, the Cancerian will refuse to say goodbye. Not every sign can cope with a Cancerian relationship, even when it's going well, because Cancerians are extremely protective of their loved ones. The more freedom-loving signs may resent having to say what time they'll be home, or will feel claustrophobic when they're continually being asked if everything's all right. To them, it's smother-love. To emotional signs, however, it can be heaven on earth.

It's a rare Cancerian who can conceal their sensitive feelings. Usually, you can't help being aware of a Cancerian's emotions because they wear their (big) hearts on their sleeves. Tears come easily to them, and they're unashamedly sentimental and nostalgic. Cancerians can find it difficult to say how they feel – they may prefer to preserve a tense or huffy silence, so they can be gently coaxed into explaining what's wrong. Sometimes, however, they may simply have taken offence. They can also be extremely defensive, automatically assuming that someone is gunning for them whatever the truth of the matter might be.

This sensitivity makes Cancerians very moody, intuitive and imaginative. They should choose their surroundings carefully because they can absorb a negative atmosphere like blotting paper. This, coupled with their natural tendency to worry, can affect Cancerians physically as well as mentally, triggering such stomach problems as indigestion and ulcers.

LEO

23 JULY – 23 AUGUST

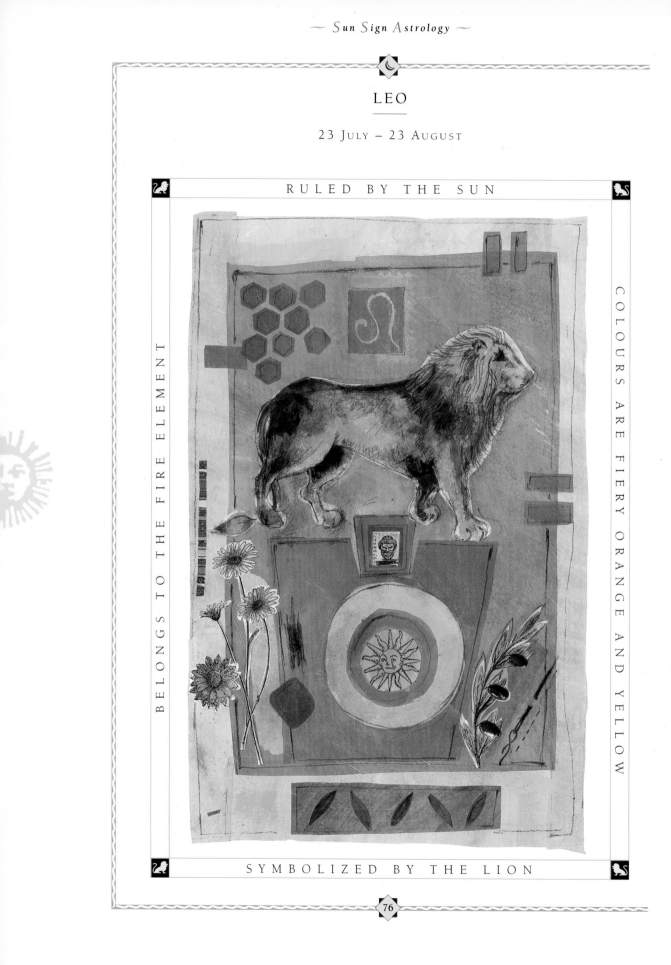

BELONGS TO THE FIRE ELEMENT

COLOURS ARE FIERY ORANGE AND YELLOW

SYMBOLIZED BY THE LION

PURRFECT! Leos are the big cats of the zodiac and, like their namesake lions, they consider themselves to be the pride of the celestial pantheon. They have an innate dignity, regality and bearing that remind you that you're not dealing with just anyone – you're dealing with a Leo.

That's because Leo is ruled by the Sun which is, after all, the centre of our solar system. Without the Sun we'd all shrivel up and die in a second, and some Leos can't help believing that the same would be true if they weren't around. These are the ones that give the rest of the sign a bad name, and they're so self-confident that you wish you could stick out a foot as they go by and trip them up.

Most Leos, it has to be said, are not like their textbook image. Not all the time, at any rate. Yes, it's true that they revel in being in the limelight and will soon start to get fidgety if they feel you're not paying them enough attention. It'll happen very subtly but you'll discover that somehow the conversation has been skilfully steered back to a subject on which the Leo can hold forth.

This may make Leos sound insufferable and overbearing, and there are certainly a few Leos who come into this category, but most of them don't. In fact, they can be extremely popular and usually have an army of devoted friends and relatives. It's difficult not to love Leos because their affectionate, generous and warm-hearted natures make them impossible to resist. They get their expansiveness and enthusiasm from their Fire element, and these traits are enhanced by the warmth from the Sun. Leos find it easy to show their emotions and can be wonderfully demonstrative.

They are also inspired present-givers, and derive enormous pleasure from choosing the perfect gift for someone. Imagine their disappointment if the gift isn't received in the right spirit or is looked at for a couple of minutes and then put to one side. Very often, the issue of giving and receiving presents is important for Leos, and may even come up in the conversation. Leos usually have very expensive tastes, but don't let this frighten you when shopping for a gift for them. Any Leo worth their salt prefers quality to quantity, so it would be far better to buy your Leo a tiny box of luxuriously expensive Belgian chocolates than a huge box of an insultingly inferior brand. They'll take it as a compliment – you obviously know that they only like the best. On the other hand, if you spend more money than you can afford, their pleasure will be marred by genuine worry that you're out of pocket.

Leo is one of the most creative signs of all, and most Leos have a strongly artistic streak. Many members of this sign come into their own the moment they step on to a stage, whether as an actor, dancer, singer, musician, impresario or anything else that takes their fancy. They're also inspired when it comes to organizational skills – if you want your office to run as smoothly as melted butter, put a Leo in charge. It's true that power goes to some Leo heads as quickly as vodka on an empty stomach, and this sign certainly has had its fair share of dictators and control freaks, but most Leos manage to avoid such excesses. They can be bossy at times, arrogant and even condescending, but somehow you always end up forgiving them because they have so many redeeming qualities.

VIRGO

24 AUGUST – 22 SEPTEMBER

SOME SIGNS ALWAYS get the fuzzy end of the lollipop when it comes to character descriptions, and Virgo usually vies with Scorpio for the dubious honour of being the weirdest sign of the lot. But is this fair?

No. It's a good thing that Virgos have a passion for tidiness and order, otherwise the rest of us would vanish beneath a pile of detritus. The world would fall apart in half an hour if every Virgo on the planet took their lunch break at the same time. Who would make things happen? Who would remind you that it's time to pay your taxes or buy some more potatoes? Virgos are reliable, meticulous, diligent, practical, pragmatic and extremely down-to-earth. You can wax lyrical to your favourite Virgo about your latest scheme, describing how wonderful it's going to be, and they'll listen in attentive silence before making a single, eminently practical comment that is the one consideration you haven't allowed for and, of course, it's the only one you should have made in the first place. That's why Virgos make such fantastic agents, accountants, advisers, assistants and general helpmeets, because they're skilled at being of service and because they remember those important little points that you've forgotten all about in your excitement. Sometimes, a Virgo can get so bogged down in detail that they lose sight of the bigger picture, which is when they need to work with a more expansive partner.

Another common Virgo problem is worry, something that Virgos have got down to a fine art. Most of them could give master classes in how to fret, feel anxious and lose sleep. They can worry themselves sick (often literally), while knowing deep down that everything will be all right. It's as if they'll worry if they haven't got anything to worry about. If you know a Virgo who suffers like this, take pity on them and encourage them to discuss their problems.

Virgos are also noted for their critical abilities. They have extremely analytical brains, which enables them to spot the flaws in other people's arguments. However, next time you're licking your wounds, remind yourself that it's much tougher being a Virgo than being a Virgo's friend, because a Virgo will be ticking themselves off virtually all day long. They're incredibly exacting and are their harshest critics.

One trait that crops up again and again when discussing Virgos is health. They're instinctively attuned to subjects connected with fitness and hygiene, and are endlessly fascinated by them, but they're the last people in the world who should read a medical encyclopedia because they'll suspect they've got everything from athlete's foot to zits.

Every Virgo should ensure they get enough rest, otherwise they can become extremely tense. Unfortunately, many Virgos find it impossible to relax. When a Virgo's digestive system starts to play up, it's a sure sign that they need to take life easy for a while.

RULED BY MERCURY

BELONGS TO THE EARTH ELEMENT

COLOURS ARE NAVY BLUE, DEEP GREEN & RICH BROWN

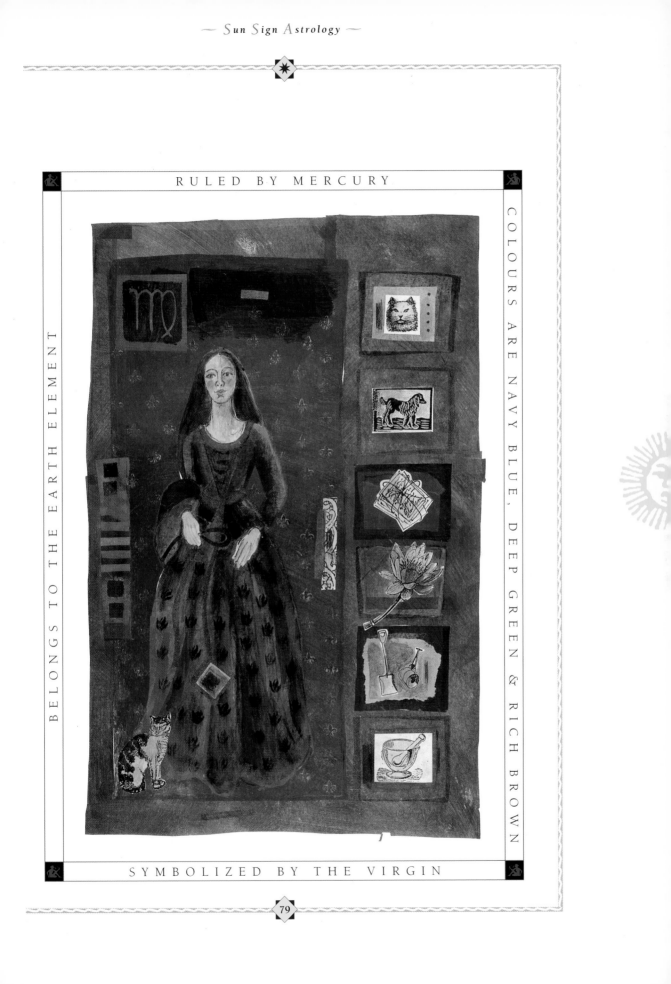

SYMBOLIZED BY THE VIRGIN

LIBRA

23 SEPTEMBER – 23 OCTOBER

RULED BY VENUS

BELONGS TO THE AIR ELEMENT

COLOURS ARE PALE PINK AND PALE BLUE

SYMBOLIZED BY THE SCALES

WE ALL NEED AT least one Libran in our lives. No other sign comes close if you're looking for someone charming, considerate, easygoing, diplomatic and understanding. Put like that, how can you resist? Librans know instinctively how to make relationships a real pleasure, how to make you feel as if you're the only person in the whole world and how to reassure you that there are still some people who understand such old-fashioned values as courtesy and politeness.

Sounds good, doesn't it? And life can certainly be great when it's graced with a few Librans. Until you try to get one to make an important decision, that is. Try it and see. That's when you discover the flip side to this person who at first sight seems too good to be true. Can a Libran make a decision? Can a cat knit? Librans are so good at seeing both sides of every argument that their natural position is to straddle the fence. They prevaricate and hedge, weighing up the pros and cons of their possible actions, until you wish they'd do something just to put everyone out of their misery. However, this apparent indecision can hide an extremely steely resolve.

Libra is the iron hand in the velvet glove, as you'll discover if you ever attempt to persuade one to do something against their will. There's no doubt that Librans often know precisely what they want; it's achieving this without upsetting anyone that's the problem. And here we have the crux of the matter – a Libran needs to feel that everyone likes them, and they'll crawl through hoops to ensure that this happens. Let's say you're going out to lunch with one, and you've arranged to meet in a wine bar. For a start, you'd better take a good book with you because the Libran will doubtless be late. When they do arrive, it will be with effusive apologies and you'll instantly forgive them. Then you'll discuss where you're going to eat. The Libran will look doubtful about everywhere you suggest, but will insist that you choose. Yet in the end you'll still wind up going to the restaurant that the Libran wanted to visit all along. They just didn't like to say so.

Luxury is very dear to any self-respecting Libran's heart. They're ruled by Venus, which predisposes them to a love of pampering, comfort and indulgence. And chocolate. Remember this next time you buy them a present.

Another area in which Librans come into their own is love. If every sign has its own destiny, then Libra's is associated with hearts and flowers, Moons and Junes. Love with a Libran can spoil you for anyone else. They'll romance you with poetry, candlelit dinners, love letters, sweetly silly gifts and heartbreaking smiles.

And they'll mean all of it. Librans are born romantics, which means they can fall in love with love. It's easy for them to get hurt because they place implicit trust and faith in the object of their desires, and they'll believe the very best of them. They'll turn a blind eye to anything coarse, ugly or unpleasant – the phrase 'rose-coloured glasses' springs to mind. When this pays off it's wonderful, but every now and then the Libran will have their heart shattered by someone who failed to live up to their high expectations. Sadly, it's a rare Libran who learns from experience, but that's one of the reasons they're so endearing, and why the rest of us keep coming back for more.

SCORPIO

24 October – 22 November

RULED BY PLUTO

BELONGS TO THE WATER ELEMENT

COLOURS ARE DEEP RED AND MAROON

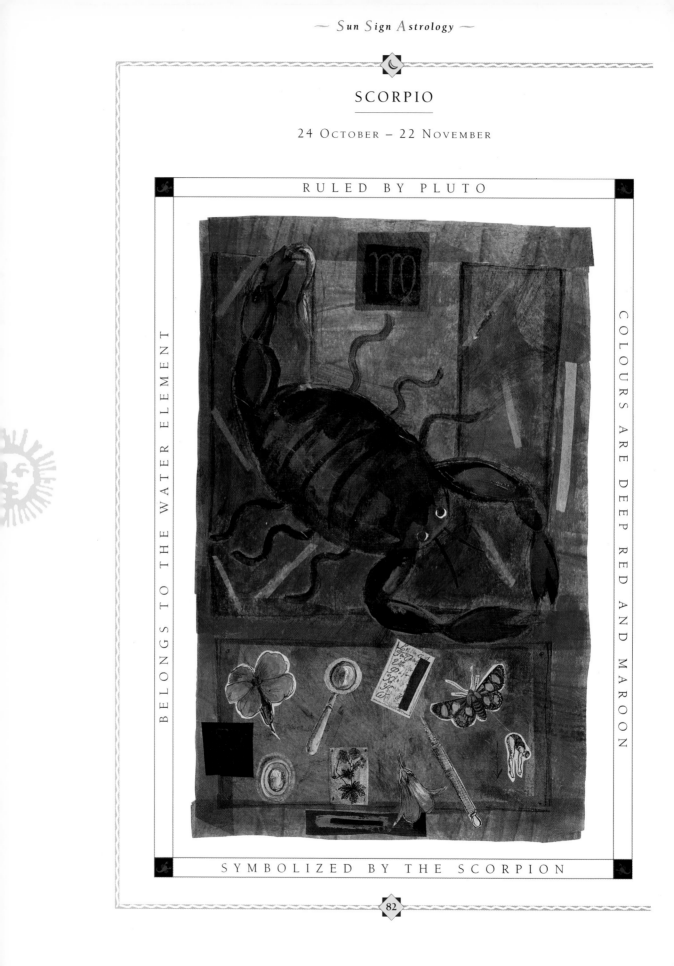

SYMBOLIZED BY THE SCORPION

SCORPIOS COMPLAIN about it all the time. Someone asks them what their sign is and, when they reply 'Scorpio' with a bright smile, the other person swallows hard and remembers a previous engagement. Why, when Scorpios are some of the best people you'll ever meet? It's because their reputation has travelled before them. Words such as 'passionate', 'intense' and 'dramatic' become translated into 'emotional volcano', 'moody' and 'power-freak' – and 'sex-mad', which is a particular bugbear for Scorpios. While all these epithets can be true at times, most Scorpios are not permanently smouldering with emotion, or if they are, they'll never let on.

If you're looking for words to explain a Scorpio, start with 'enigmatic' and 'mysterious'. Scorpios operate on an emotional level, but it's not one that's comfortably expressed or easily accessible. It can even be difficult for a Scorpio themselves to come to terms with their intense emotions because they run so deep and they're so complex. Very often, something so dark and painful lurks at the core of their feelings that the Scorpio is loath to investigate, and they certainly won't want anyone else to pry into the innermost recesses of their heart. That's not to say that Scorpios can't have decent relationships, because they make wonderful partners and lifelong friends. But certain areas of a Scorpio's life are off-limits, even to themselves.

Another of those Scorpio words is 'passionate', and that's certainly true. However, they won't only be passionate in the bedroom. They're passionate about everything that means a lot to them, from their hobbies to their favourite piece of music. Life without passion would be pretty bland to a Scorpio. They need to feel emotionally involved with whatever they're doing, so a Scorpio who's bored by their job or their partner is very unhappy. Are they jealous? Yes. When sufficiently provoked (which sometimes isn't saying much) they can be possessive and suspicious, convinced that you're up to no good or are deceiving them behind their backs. It's one of those astrological curiosities that Scorpios often choose other Scorpios as partners – no doubt because they understand one another's emotional depths.

Although Scorpios may be reluctant to reveal their feelings, they're extremely sensitive and can be easily hurt. You won't know what you've done, but you'll be aware of a nasty atmosphere and possibly even sulking. Many Scorpios are highly intuitive and psychic, which is something they either embrace with wholehearted enthusiasm or shy away from completely. There are no half-measures for Scorpios.

Perhaps because they're surrounded by such an enticing sense of mystery, Scorpios are blessed with extremely magnetic personalities. They also have a wonderful, earthy sense of humour which helps them to appreciate the lighter side of life and which gets them through the bad times. Some signs seem to trip through life relatively unscathed, but that isn't the case for Scorpios. They often carry deep emotional scars or have experienced dramatic twists of fate. Scorpios seem to live their lives in distinct chapters – you can almost see the demarcation line between one episode in their life and the next. When things become unendurable, they simply end that relationship or experience and move on to the next.

SAGITTARIUS

23 November – 21 December

SAGITTARIANS ARE THE great optimists of the zodiac. Their glasses are always half-full and their clouds always have silver linings. And they're usually right. It can drive the more prudent signs mad. There's a Sagittarian, practically asking for trouble, taking chances and over-committing themselves, yet they usually manage to pull the rabbit out of the hat. They're a walking advert for the power of positive thinking.

Challenges are meat and drink to a Sagittarian. Whoever first said that they can do the impossible in a day but miracles take a little longer must have been a Sagittarian. Of course, sometimes they fall flat on their face when they overestimate their capabilities but, like one of those bouncy toys you can't knock over, they'll always recover. Will they have learned from the experience? Probably not, although it's also true that Sagittarius is the most philosophical sign of the zodiac. This is the sign of the teacher, the sage and the prophet, and most Sagittarians have a very wise streak even if they do combine it with a (sometimes foolhardy) love of taking risks. They regard knowledge as an essential ingredient of civilization, and spend their lives broadening their own education, whether that's in a formal way or simply by absorbing facts as they go along.

Any self-respecting Sagittarian has a house full of books which reflect all their passing enthusiasms, from quilting to teaching themselves a foreign language; Sagittarians can become completely wrapped up in an idea or pastime, and will buy everything they can on the subject, then abandon it when the next passion comes along.

So always head for the nearest Sagittarian when you're looking for the answer to any kind of question. This love of knowledge makes Sagittarians fascinating companions but sometimes they become so sold on an idea that they feel duty-bound to convert everyone around them. Although most Sagittarians are refreshingly open-minded, there are a few who become blinkered, dogmatic proselytizers. A case of 'have soapbox, will travel'.

Speaking of travel, most Sagittarians were born with the wind in their hair. They love to keep on the move, whether mentally or physically. While some Sagittarians enjoy donning a backpack and disappearing into the wide blue yonder, others are quite happy to indulge in armchair travel. Of course, it's difficult to travel when you have family commitments, but Sagittarians love to think that they're free spirits who can go wherever they choose, whenever they want. Sometimes this causes major problems in relationships because Sagittarians are so wary of emotional commitment. Plenty of them are happily married but they do still dream of being

young, free and single. That Sagittarian restlessness will never leave them.

Another Sagittarian preoccupation is honesty. In fact, they're so concerned with telling the truth that they can decimate your feelings in the process. They'd never dream of hurting you intentionally but they have to tell it like it is. So you'd better be prepared.

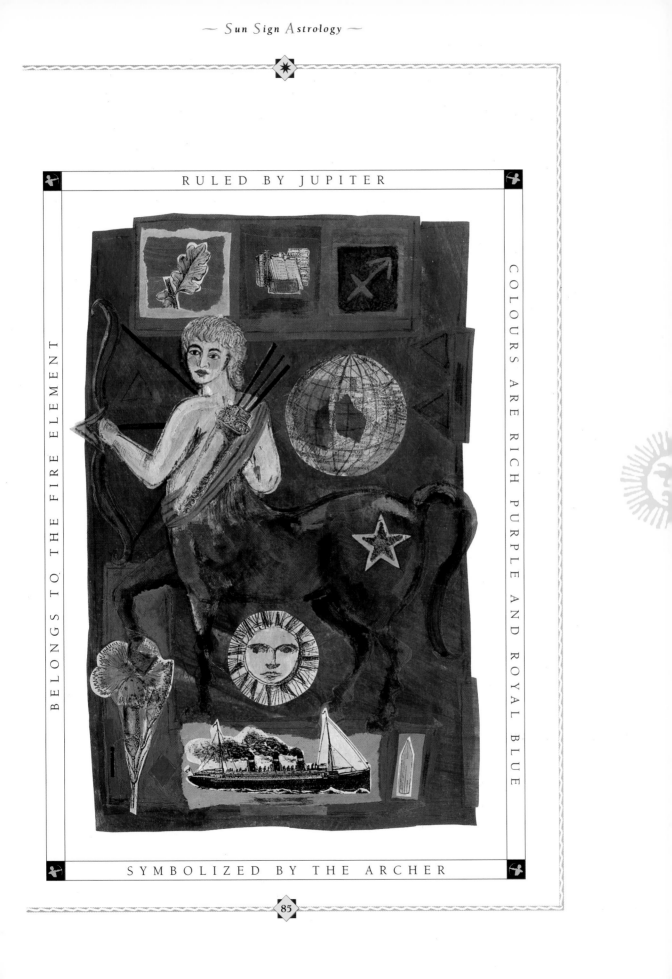

CAPRICORN

22 December – 20 January

RULED BY SATURN

BELONGS TO THE EARTH ELEMENT

COLOURS ARE DARK GREY, BROWN AND BLACK

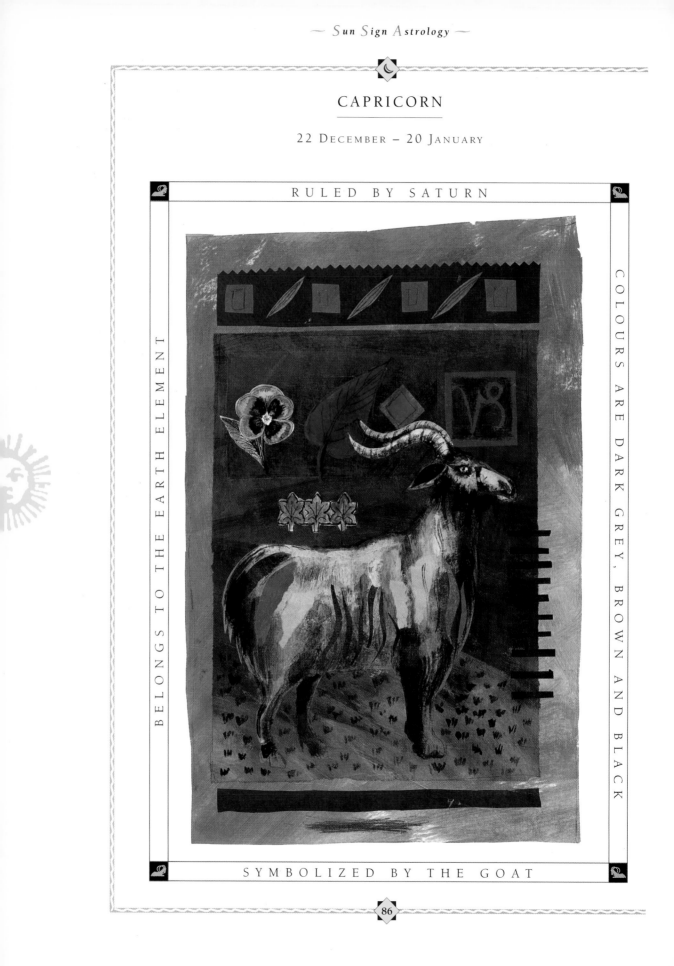

SYMBOLIZED BY THE GOAT

ATLAS CARRIED THE WORLD on his shoulders; and Capricorns carry the cares of the world on theirs. Their tremendous sense of responsibility makes them utterly reliable and steadfast, trustworthy and stable. Yet this can be a curse as well as a blessing, partly because Capricorns have to do the job properly – they spend inordinate amounts of time making sure that everything is done to the best of their ability. They don't know the meaning of the word 'delegation', neglecting their personal lives as they build up a career. They'll bring work home, alienating their loved ones in the process. They are workaholics.

Capricorns are deeply concerned about what other people think of them. This need to be respected and admired can stop them relaxing because they always feel they should be up to the mark and on good form. Success is also extremely important to them, and they need to feel they've achieved something with their lives. This is relative, of course – one Capricorn will dream of making a career in banking while another will long for a successful family life – but, nevertheless, Capricorns are always aiming for particular goals. And they won't relax until they achieve them, at which point they'll create a whole new set of objectives. And so it goes on.

They've got Saturn, that stern old taskmaster of the zodiac, to thank for this dutiful, respectable and hard-working attitude. Saturn instils in them the need for achievement and the desire to learn from experience. It's also why youthful Capricorns have old heads on young shoulders. Calamities and setbacks that would floor some

signs are simply grist to the Capricorn mill. Yes, they'll feel depressed at the time but they'll soon brush the dust of life's failures off their beautifully tailored clothes and carry on regardless.

Depression is a very Capricorn state of mind. Capricorns are predisposed, like Eeyore in *Winnie the Pooh*, to look on the gloomy side of life. They like to think that this makes them realistic, preventing them from having their hopes raised only for them to be dashed later on, but actually all it does is make them miserable. Some Capricorns can even secretly derive a strange satisfaction from being unhappy.

Yet this doesn't mean that Capricorns aren't good fun or that they continually drag themselves around like a wet weekend. On the contrary, they're among the best rabble-rousers of the zodiac and they certainly know how to have a good time. They may drink the deepest and eat the most heartily when someone else is picking up the bill, but that's understandable when you realize that Saturn acts as a brake on everything they do, including spending money. They also have a delightfully dry sense of humour, especially when they are laughing at themselves.

Emotional reserve often gets in the way of a Capricorn and their nearest and dearest. They may feel love deeply but it's difficult for them to show it. Of all the signs, Capricorns are the least demonstrative, especially in public. They may act unconcerned and rather remote, yet they'll turn pink with pleasure when you pay them a compliment or give them a hug. The best way to deal with this is to keep giving them plenty of hugs, in hopes that they'll eventually get used to the idea.

AQUARIUS

21 JANUARY – 18 FEBRUARY

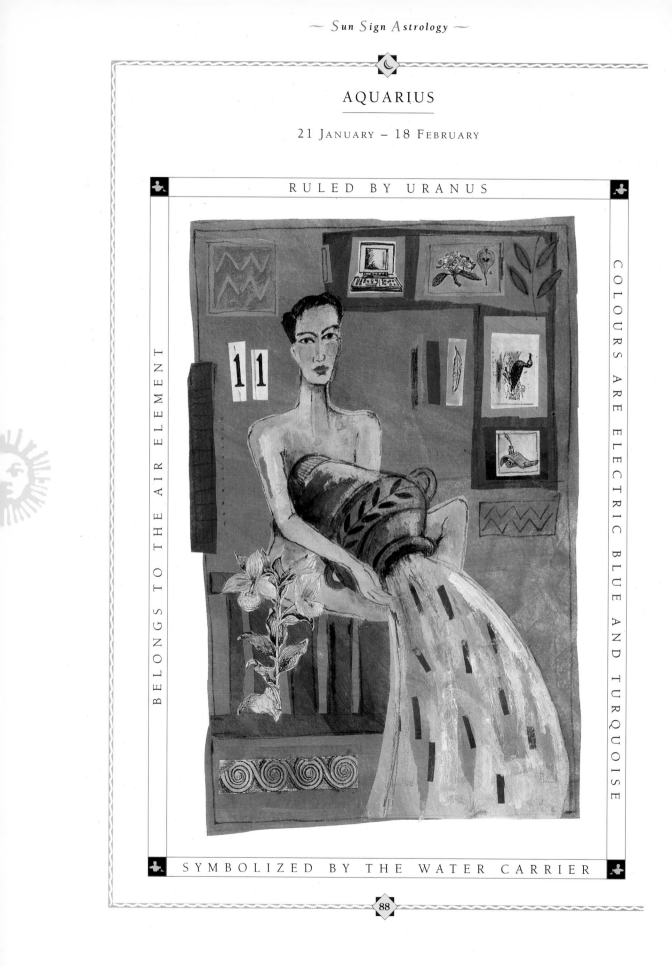

RULED BY URANUS

BELONGS TO THE AIR ELEMENT

COLOURS ARE ELECTRIC BLUE AND TURQUOISE

SYMBOLIZED BY THE WATER CARRIER

AQUARIANS defy all attempt at description. They're a law unto themselves, and are like no other sign. This is what makes them so fascinating, because you haven't a clue where you are with them. They can be the most far-sighted, understanding and open-minded people you've ever met and it'll be a pleasure to talk to them; half an hour later they've turned into such radical, intolerant and obdurate maniacs that you're left speechless. What happened?

In a word, Uranus. This planet rules Aquarius and represents revolution, sudden change and disruption. Once you understand this, you'll begin to gain an insight into the Aquarians you know. For a start, they're complete iconoclasts who are astrologically programmed to challenge shibboleths, uncover hypocrisy and kick down the doors of convention. A true Aquarian is in the vanguard, spearheading new movements and making pronouncements that are way ahead of their time. Aquarians have no truck with the notion of following tradition for its own sake. 'Why?' the Aquarian will ask, and it's an unanswerable question.

Aquarians are intellectually motivated. They approach the world in a highly logical, rational and unemotional way and are most comfortable when dealing with the realms of thought and ideas. Such tricky subjects as their emotions, however, can have them stumped. They're happy to discuss the concept of emotion, turning it into an intellectual exercise but actually dealing with the way they feel can be extremely difficult.

So it's hardly surprising that Aquarius is the most independent sign of the zodiac. If you want to maintain a balanced relationship with an Aquarian you must learn never to question their desire for freedom, and you must never appear to cling. This may mean that you have to wear boxing gloves in order to prevent yourself dialling the Aquarian's phone number whenever they're not around, but that's just the way it is.

This dogmatic streak is their Achilles heel. When an Aquarian reaches a decision or forms an opinion, hell will freeze over before they change their minds. Or before they admit to doing so, at any rate – goodness knows what's going on in that Aquarian brain. They can also take immense delight in being contrary, contumacious, idiosyncratic and downright awkward.

Given this mulish streak, why would anyone want to know an Aquarian, unless they're another Aquarian? Because they're funny, loyal, original, sparkling, fascinating, charismatic and they make wonderfully faithful and loving friends. You can

count on an Aquarian to tell you the truth (though, once they have, you may wish they hadn't). If you ask them what they think of your new outfit, and they believe it makes you look like something that's been left out in the rain, that's what you'll be told.

Another truly magnificent Aquarian trait is their humanitarian attitude. They loathe bigotry and believe in accepting people for what they are, rather than for what they're wearing or the colour of their skin. They view life very clearly, and often from a perspective that's blindingly obvious once they explain it yet which had escaped you until that moment. Aquarians are the custodians of our future, the gatekeepers of our destiny and the great thinkers of the zodiac. Your life is richer for knowing them.

PISCES

19 FEBRUARY – 20 MARCH

Pisces is the last of the Water signs and the twelfth sign in the zodiac, which puts this sign in a privileged position. Some people believe that one's final incarnation on earth is as a Piscean.

There is certainly something otherworldly about Pisceans. They are capable of extraordinary compassion, sympathy and understanding, making them the nearest thing we have to living saints, although it has to be said that this high-mindedness can turn into martyrdom. That's because Pisces is ruled by Neptune, the planet of mystery, escapism and deception. So a Piscean may think they're being completely selfless when actually they're on a huge ego trip.

Such self-deception is perhaps the biggest potential pitfall for a Piscean. They are often extremely reluctant to face unpleasant truths and will therefore expend a great deal of energy in turning a blind eye to unpalatable facts, no matter how obvious these are to everyone else. They can also be gullible and are easily led – this is the classic Sun sign of the drug-taker and alcoholic because Neptune can dramatically deplete the willpower. Pisceans can be either the saint or the sinner, and many manage to accomplish both.

A Piscean's emotions are always close to the surface. They have big hearts and are easily moved to tears by anything from hideous news items to sentimental

films. Most have strong intuitions and many are psychic although some deliberately stifle this ability. With their powerful imaginations, they are very creative and artistic, but can sometimes magnify small worries out of all proportion.

Gifted dancers, Pisceans also excel in professions connected with the cinema, cosmetics, fashion (many Pisceans radiate glamour) and the oil industry. The caring professions attract many Pisceans.

Their compassionate and romantic natures mean that Pisceans are wholehearted partners, putting everything they've got into the relationship. Unfortunately, they may put their partner on an impossibly high pedestal or refuse to acknowledge difficulties when they arise – Pisceans have got wearing rose-tinted spectacles down to a fine art.

When it comes to health, Pisceans may have problems with their feet. Generally, Pisceans are not the most physically robust of signs because their emotions can have such a powerful and disruptive effect on their health – many of their illnesses and ailments may be emotionally based. Pisceans can soak up the atmosphere around them, so should aim to spend as much time as possible in amenable surroundings.

Many Pisceans are instinctively drawn to water, especially when they're in need of peace or succour. They may enjoy swimming or taking long, relaxing baths, and derive much solace from walking along a riverbank, lake or seashore. They'll truly feel in their element.

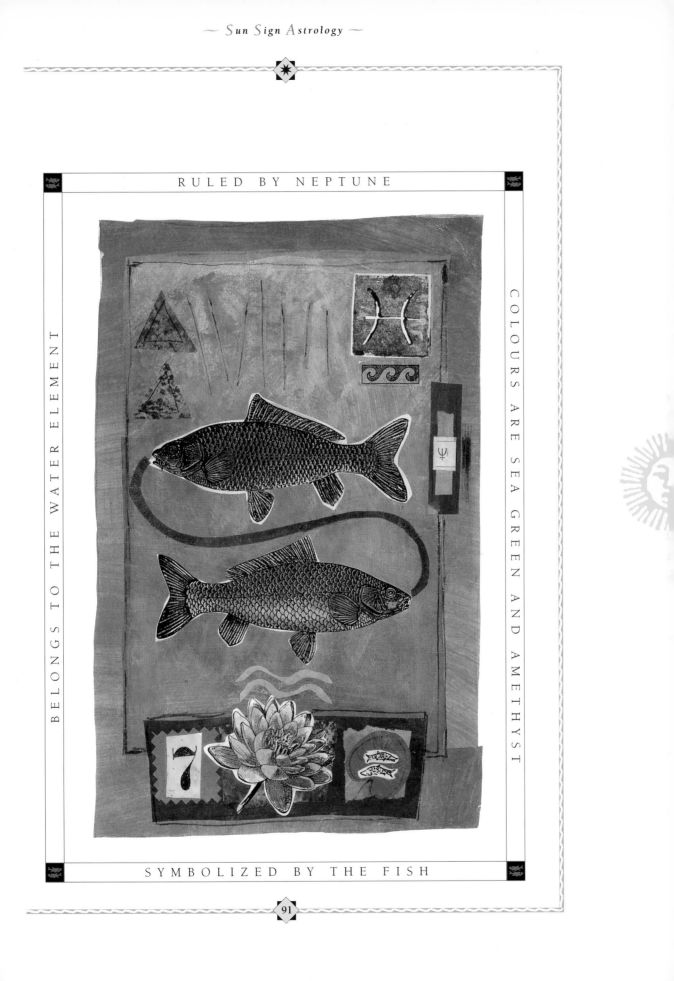

COMPATIBILITY IN LOVE AND SEX

WOMAN / MAN	ARIES	TAURUS	GEMINI	CANCER	LEO	VIRGO
ARIES	Sexy, racy, hot-blooded	Tricky, avoid jealous scenes	Good fun, lively	Competitive but sexy	Vibrant, exciting	Difficult – take care
TAURUS	Steady, loyal	Safe, sensual	Difficult	Lovely, cosy	Sensual but expect rows	Supportive, sexy
GEMINI	Dynamic, exciting	Do you understand each other?	All talk and no action!	At emotional odds	Expensive but fantastic	Chatty and unemotional
CANCER	You could hurt each other	Blissful, earthy	Not much in common	Cosy but moody	Leo wears the trousers	Emotion versus reason
LEO	You were made for each other!	Hot-blooded	Terrific fun	Tender, kind	Sexy, ego clashes	Hard work
VIRGO	Are you sure about this?	Carnal	Lively, light-hearted	You'll need to work hard	Difficult	Either great or awful
LIBRA	Vibrant, good fun	Hedonistic, sybaritic	You'll hit the heights	You share the same goals	Fun-loving but pricey	Awkward
SCORPIO	Erotic, hot-blooded	Dramatic, sexy	Handle with care	Spicy, lustful	Watch those rows!	Great in bed
SAGITTARIUS	Ardent	You're too different	Bingo!	Nothing in common	Flashy, good fun	Lots of talk
CAPRICORN	Hot stuff	Enjoy!	Emotions too diverse	Heaven on earth	Very showy	Stable emotions
AQUARIUS	A lot of fun	Aquarius could feel trapped	You've both met your match!	You're too different	Fantastic!	Too analytical for love
PISCES	Take care, Pisces!	Pisces could feel stifled	Too much like hard work	Ten out of ten	Steamy	Full of potential
MAN / WOMAN	ARIES	TAURUS	GEMINI	CANCER	LEO	VIRGO

LIBRA	SCORPIO	SAGITTARIUS	CAPRICORN	AQUARIUS	PISCES	WOMAN / MAN
Exciting	Intense, passionate	Entertaining, lively	Great if you share a goal	Chatty, dynamic	You're at emotional cross-purposes	ARIES
Enjoyable but expensive	Hot-blooded but possessive	Freedom versus stability	Practical but raunchy	Dogmatic, difficult	Sensitive, loving	TAURUS
Intoxicating, loving	Awkward and painful	Terrific	Could be emotionally painful	The best of friends	Be kind to each other	GEMINI
A great team!	Feelings run very deep	Nothing in common	Marvellous, satisfying	For masochists only	Loving, emotional	CANCER
Enormous fun	A clash of egos	Exciting, great for travel	A very showy couple	Sparkling, dynamic	Full of affection	LEO
OK for a while	Raunchy and earthy	Great for a fling	One of the all-time greats	Critical of each other	Has the potential to hurt	VIRGO
Romantic but indecisive	Not much in common	You could get hurt	A fantastic team	Lively but tense	Sweet and loving	LIBRA
Too intense for Libra	Very hot stuff, intense	Painful for Scorpio	Very raunchy	Chalk and cheese	Feelings run high	SCORPIO
You intrigue each other	Brief encounter only	Freewheeling, great friends	Too much like hard work	You fascinate each other	Pisces could get hurt	SAGITTARIUS
You share many interests	Very powerful	Is it worth the trouble?	Serious but satisfying	Either terrific or terrible	Take it gently	CAPRICORN
Libra will tame Aquarius	Sparring partners	Two free spirits together	Loosen up, Capricorn!	Best friends	Too many differences	AQUARIUS
Romance all the way	Lots of passion	Pisces could get hurt	Very good indeed	Emotions versus logic	Highly emotional	PISCES
LIBRA	SCORPIO	SAGITTARIUS	CAPRICORN	AQUARIUS	PISCES	MAN / WOMAN

COMPATIBILITY IN BUSINESS

WOMAN / MAN	ARIES	TAURUS	GEMINI	CANCER	LEO	VIRGO
ARIES	Highly competitive	Aries talks, Taurus works	Full of great ideas	Plenty of drive	There'll be no stopping you	Too much trouble
TAURUS	Very successful	Don't get stuck in a rut	Do you understand each other?	Magnificent	Tense at times	Great!
GEMINI	What a double act!	Gemini will make things happen	Dazzling!	You're too different	Dynamic	Terrific together
CANCER	Very ambitious	You'll take care of each other	Awkward	Terrific!	Agree to differ	You'll annoy each other
LEO	Lively and fiery	Big ego clashes	Great fun	Leo will get impatient	Sort out who's the boss	Not easy
VIRGO	You're too different	You'll achieve a lot	A great team	Too much effort needed	The odd couple!	Don't work too hard
LIBRA	Exciting	Enjoyable	You'll like each other a lot	A lot of fun	Most impressive	Take it one step at a time
SCORPIO	Sparks will fly	Gutsy and great	It'll be love or hate	Cancer could feel threatened	Scorpio mustn't keep secrets	You'll help each other
SAGITTARIUS	Dynamic	Not a happy couple	Most enjoyable	Very difficult	Marvellous	Divide the work up evenly
CAPRICORN	Two high fliers!	You'll work long and hard	You don't understand each other	A powerful team	You'll boss each other about	Excellent
AQUARIUS	You'll give as good as you get	Neither of you will back down	Lots of fun	Cancer will find it hard-going	Learn to give and take	A good team
PISCES	Nothing in common	A good team	Enjoyable	A great pairing	Uneasy at times	You'll spur each other on
MAN / WOMAN	ARIES	TAURUS	GEMINI	CANCER	LEO	VIRGO

	LIBRA	SCORPIO	SAGITTARIUS	CAPRICORN	AQUARIUS	PISCES	WOMAN / MAN
ARIES	Punchy and good fun	Lots of drive and power	A great team	You'll really go places	Expect ego clashes	Aries may be too bossy	
TAURUS	Taurus will work harder than Libra	Opposites attract	You'll drive each other mad	You'll achieve a lot	Work with, not against, each other	Good fun	
GEMINI	Highly enjoyable	Weird but it could work	A lot of laughs	You'll impress each other	The ideas will flow	Really good	
CANCER	You share the same goals	Highly-charged	Do you share the same aims?	Most enjoyable	You have nothing in common	Friendly and fun	
LEO	Sparky and dynamic	Beware battles for power	Lots of expenses!	Very hard-working	The dream team	It could work	
VIRGO	Libra will help Virgo relax	Not bad!	Great minds think alike	Powerful	You'll nag each other	Virgo will organize Pisces	
LIBRA	Hard to make decisions	Not enough in common	Full of good ideas	Fantastic	Inventive and exciting	The charm offensive!	
SCORPIO	Awkward	What a team!	Not a happy pair	Scorpio will dominate	Too many rows	Highly-charged	
SAGITTARIUS	Good fun	Tense	Inspired!	Nothing in common	Terrific!	You'll inspire each other	
CAPRICORN	You're good for each other	You'll work hard	Oil and water	You can't fail	Better than you imagine	Could be tough for Pisces	
AQUARIUS	Great for ideas	Volatile	You'll respect each other	Tradition versus new ideas	Way ahead of your time	Difficult	
PISCES	Very civilized	Intuitive	Exciting!	Can Pisces stand the pace?	No common ground	Keep your feet on the ground	MAN / WOMAN

Chinese
Astrology

Chinese astrology is based on the lunar calendar. Each

Chinese sign lasts more or less for a year, beginning

with the New Moon in the sign of Aquarius. This New

Moon can fall any time between early January and late

February, so if you were born during this time, check

carefully to see which sign you belong to. According

to Chinese tradition, the signs were given their

names by Buddha, five centuries before the birth of

Christ. As Buddha lay dying he asked all the animals in the

world to visit him and say farewell. Only twelve did so, and to thank

them he offered each one their own year, so they would become immortal.

RAT

IN THE WEST, it's a term of abuse to call some-one a rat, but no such stigma applies in the East. There, the Rat is a very different crea-ture, being the first sign of the Chinese zodiac. He must have been pretty quick off the mark to be the first animal that answered the summons of the dying Buddha (which is how the zodiac was assembled), and the Chinese have admired his character ever since.

Rats are easily iden-tified. They are the ones surrounded by a crowd of people. These could be adoring friends, dot-ing relatives or indus-trious colleagues, but there they'll all be, with the Rat happily occupy-ing centre-stage and doing all the talking. If things are going badly for a Rat, they'll seek out a sympathetic ear and pour out their heart. If things are going well, they'll get on the phone and tell everyone. And if things are just ticking over, the Rat will have something to say about that too.

Perhaps it's just as well that Rats are so charm-ing, because they can get away with conversa-tional murder. (If you want to know the very latest gossip, you now know who to ask.) They're also extremely friendly and outgoing. The Rat sense of humour wins them many fans, and it can be their saving grace sometimes because they're able to laugh at themselves. This blessing stands them in particularly good stead when they're guilty of interfering in other people's lives. This isn't bossiness – well, not exactly. It's simply that the Rat will make certain suggestions and, before

31 January 1900 – 18 February 1901
18 February 1912 – 5 February 1913
5 February 1924 – 24 January 1925
24 January 1936 – 10 February 1937
10 February 1948 – 28 January 1949
28 January 1960 – 14 February 1961
15 February 1972 – 2 February 1973
2 February 1984 – 19 February 1985
19 February 1996 – 6 February 1997
7 February 2008 – 25 January 2009

you know what's happened, you'll be carrying them out to the letter. And if you're a bit slow off the mark, the Rat will exercise a gentle persis-tence until it seems easier to get the job done than to be reminded yet again.

Rats have excellent intellects and enjoy putting them to good use. They have wide-ranging inter-ests and they're always being swept along by a new enthusiasm. This may last for several years or equally it could fizzle out in a few days, but the Rat will still pursue it with devotion in the meantime.

Money is always a most important subject for Rats. They adore having money to burn but they also live in fear of not having enough in the bank for a rainy day, so they try to ensure they have the best of both worlds by fluctuating wildly between extrava-gance and avarice. Watch a Rat on a spending spree and you'll see a flurry of carrier bags, credit cards, cheques and banknotes flying in all direc-tions. Yet this same Rat that you saw flinging money about will balk at the price of a cappuc-cino in one café and take a ten-minute walk in order to buy it cheaper somewhere else. The cap-puccino won't taste nearly as nice, of course, but the Rat will be delighted to know they saved a few pennies.

Each sign fares well in some years and not in others. Rats flourish in Rat, Dragon and Monkey years, but have to scrabble about in Rabbit, Horse and Rooster years.

OX

DEPENDABLE AND RELIABLE, Oxen are the work-force of the Chinese zodiac. Given their name, you couldn't really expect anything else. While other signs may make a big song and dance about getting things done or achieving their goals, Oxen simply apply their noses to the grindstone and do whatever is necessary. This devotion to duty can mean that Oxen plough a lonely furrow through life, partly because they're so single-minded about fulfilling their ambitions and partly because they do take life rather seriously. When they're at their most strict, they can be sticklers for convention and arch traditionalists, greeting new ideas with a dismissive, seen-it-all-before shrug of the shoulders and a look that says, 'You'll learn'.

Oxen believe that if things are worth doing, they're worth doing well – and also that you probably can't trust anyone else to do them because they'll only make a hash of everything. That's how Oxen end up burning the candle at both ends and becoming exhausted (but highly successful) workaholics with scant social life and a family who only recognize them from their photos.

Oxen are capable of immense sacrifice, especially if it's in a good cause – their career, for a start. Success is extremely important to them, because they need to know they're admired in the eyes of the world. Oxen have no patience with people who aren't prepared to work hard for the things they want in life, and can even be quite moralistic and rigid about anyone who fails to live up to their own high standards. Yet they can be wonderfully, tear-inducingly kind when you really need them.

Oxen are extremely down-to-earth – literally. They're keen and gifted gardeners but, even if they don't have their own patch of earth to tend, they appreciate the beauties of nature and benefit from stopping work every now and then and wandering through the great outdoors. Oxen need to take time to smell the roses. It's vital to their well-being, so if you're looking for a present for your favourite Ox, you could consider a pot plant or Bonsai tree to sit on their desk. If you're looking for romance, Oxen don't fit the bill. To be honest, they don't even come close. Although they're excellent providers for their families, it's quite another matter for them to let you know how they feel about you. Declarations of love? Romantic candlelit dinners for two? Dream on! Oxen are the strong and silent types. They'll get more worked up about the performance of their stocks and shares than they will about the way you make them feel, but that doesn't mean they're incapable of emotion. Far from it. It's simply that showing it would be making a spectacle of themselves, and they would never do that.

Each sign fares better in some years than others. Oxen find life plentiful in Ox, Snake and Rooster years, but endure slim pickings in Goat, Dragon and Dog years.

19 FEBRUARY 1901 – 7 FEBRUARY 1902
6 FEBRUARY 1913 – 25 JANUARY 1914
25 JANUARY 1925 – 12 FEBRUARY 1926
11 FEBRUARY 1937 – 30 JANUARY 1938
29 JANUARY 1949 – 16 FEBRUARY 1950
15 FEBRUARY 1961 – 4 FEBRUARY 1962
3 FEBRUARY 1973 – 22 JANUARY 1974
20 FEBRUARY 1985 – 8 FEBRUARY 1986
7 FEBRUARY 1997 – 27 JANUARY 1998
26 JANUARY 2009 – 13 FEBRUARY 2010

TIGER

TRADITIONAL CHINESE astrology claims that Tigers are able to ward off ghosts, fire and thieves, so you know who to turn to next time you're bothered by any of these nuisances. Perhaps it's because they have very loud roars that will frighten off anything within reach and also extinguish any flames at the same time. Not that you can always count on them to behave like this, because Tigers are nothing if not unpredictable creatures.

They are also very colourful. They light up your life in all sorts of ways, but particularly when they are feeling active and adventurous, and want to take you along for the ride. They are not above taking some pretty foolhardy risks too (foolhardy to anyone who wasn't born a Tiger, that is), and two of their favourite pursuits are driving fast cars and indulging in a spot of gambling. If the gambling pays off, that's great and you'll both have fun spending their winnings, but if it doesn't the Tiger will always live to fight another day. Perhaps it's just as well that Tigers are one of the luckiest signs in the Chinese zodiac, and they always seem to land on their feet. Otherwise, goodness knows what would happen. This can seem quite unfair to some of the more conservative-minded signs who believe in living by the rules and doing their very best at all times. Tigers believe that rules are made to be broken and they know that they've got at least nine lives, if not several more, tucked up their sleeves.

8 FEBRUARY 1902 – 28 JANUARY 1903
26 JANUARY 1914 – 13 FEBRUARY 1915
13 FEBRUARY 1926 – 1 FEBRUARY 1927
31 JANUARY 1938 – 18 FEBRUARY 1939
17 FEBRUARY 1950 – 5 FEBRUARY 1951
5 FEBRUARY 1962 – 24 JANUARY 1963
23 JANUARY 1974 – 10 FEBRUARY 1975
9 FEBRUARY 1986 – 28 JANUARY 1987
28 JANUARY 1998 – 15 FEBRUARY 1999
14 FEBRUARY 2010 – 2 FEBRUARY 2011

As you might expect from a sign named after one of the most attractive animals of all, Tigers set great store by their appearance. This can make them vain (say it quietly – you don't want to set off a Tigerish roar), so that whenever you want to look in the mirror they're always in the way, but it also gives them a certain style all of their own. These people know how to dress, putting together outfits that really suit them and which make them stand out from the crowd. They dare to be different, and it works.

Tigers hate to think that the grass is growing under their feet or that they're getting stuck in a rut. They'll do anything to avoid this, so it can be difficult to keep up with them. Some Tigers change jobs as often as you change your socks, and it's not uncommon to find Tigers who've worked in several different professions during the course of their remarkable lives. This may mean that a Tiger doesn't reach the position of authority for which nature intended them, because they've never managed to stick to one profession for long enough, but that won't bother them. And if a job doesn't work out properly, so what? They'll simply find another one. And they usually do, even if it's against the odds. But, of course, Tigers adore betting on long odds.

Each sign fares well in some years and struggles in others. Tigers have a rip-roaring time in Tiger, Horse and Dog years, but have less to celebrate in Monkey, Pig and Snake years.

RABBIT

IN CHINESE ASTROLOGY, the Rabbit symbolizes immortality. Could this have something to do with the remarkable breeding qualities of its animal counterpart? Or is it because Rabbits are renowned survivors, quietly picking themselves up from the ruins whenever life lets them down, and then getting on with the business of recouping their losses?

If you have just met a Rabbit and you want to know a short-cut to their heart, it's very simple. Flatter them by buying them something that's very high-quality. Even when a Rabbit can barely scrape by on their annual income, they'll still spend a vast proportion of their budget on the best clothes and accessories they can possibly afford. Sometimes they simply can't afford them but they'll buy them anyway. If you've ever wondered what kind of person orders hand-made shoes, bespoke suits and couture clothes, it's a Rabbit.

Beauty is extremely important to these creatures. They can endure all kinds of hardship provided their surroundings are congenial, harmonious and comfortable. What they can't abide is untidiness and rooms where every available surface is covered with half-read newspapers, buttons that have fallen off shirts and letters waiting to be answered. The Rabbit will endure things for so long, before sweeping the whole mess into a heap and throwing it out. On second thoughts, they'll leave it for you to throw out.

29 JANUARY 1903 – 15 FEBRUARY 1904
14 FEBRUARY 1915 – 2 FEBRUARY 1916
2 FEBRUARY 1927 – 22 JANUARY 1928
19 FEBRUARY 1939 – 7 FEBRUARY 1940
6 FEBRUARY 1951 – 26 JANUARY 1952
25 JANUARY 1963 – 12 FEBRUARY 1964
11 FEBRUARY 1975 – 30 JANUARY 1976
29 JANUARY 1987 – 16 FEBRUARY 1988
16 FEBRUARY 1999 – 4 FEBRUARY 2000
3 FEBRUARY 2011 – 22 JANUARY 2012

After all, you created it, didn't you? Not that they'll do this in a confrontational way, because they loathe rows. They'll just pile everything in a heap in a place where you can't fail to miss it.

Culture is another essential element of a Rabbit's life. Rabbits appreciate fine art, literature, music, the dramatic arts and anything else of that ilk that makes their lives worth living. However, they're curiously reluctant to join the queue to see the latest art exhibition or film. They hate the thought of having to negotiate crowds because they feel quite uncomfortable whenever they are surrounded by too many people.

Rabbits really come into their own when doing the washing up. Both sexes are sticklers for squeaky-clean plates and glasses, and practically rub off the pattern on your favourite china in their efforts to get it clean. They're also past masters at providing comfort and solace when things go wrong for you. This is when they really come into their own, because they'll listen carefully and make extremely helpful suggestions. Mind you, they aren't above a little plain-speaking, especially if they think you've made a slip-up or you aren't being honest with yourself, but you'll have to take the small helping of rough with the large dollops of smooth.

Each sign fares well in some years and not in others. Rabbits have spring fever in Rabbit, Goat and Pig years, but life is low-key in Rooster, Horse and Rat years.

DRAGON

DRAGONS MORE THAN live up to their name. If you annoy one, it won't be long before they start breathing fire, stamping their feet and swishing their tails about. You can expect sparks to fly, and you'll be left in no doubt that you've transgressed in some way. They don't mince their words, which is why so many people are rather wary of the Dragons in their life.

Hearing this will make any self-respecting Dragon raise their eyebrows in bewilderment, before they shake their heads in resignation over the ridiculously sensitive natures of the people they know. My goodness, they'll ask, what's wrong with a person handing out a little honest advice every now and then?

16 FEBRUARY 1904 – 3 FEBRUARY 1905
3 FEBRUARY 1916 – 22 JANUARY 1917
23 JANUARY 1928 – 9 FEBRUARY 1929
8 FEBRUARY 1940 – 26 JANUARY 1941
27 JANUARY 1952 – 13 FEBRUARY 1953
13 FEBRUARY 1964 – 1 FEBRUARY 1965
31 JANUARY 1976 – 17 FEBRUARY 1977
17 FEBRUARY 1988 – 5 FEBRUARY 1989
5 FEBRUARY 2000 – 23 JANUARY 2001
23 JANUARY 2012 – 9 FEBRUARY 2013

Nothing, you'll reply, it's simply that the Dragon brand of advice ought to come with a government health warning. If you're foolish enough to attempt a discussion with a Dragon on a subject they feel strongly about or find offensive (Dragons are quite prudish), you really ought to wear a suit of armour, just in case. Otherwise, such Dragon comments as 'you don't know what you're talking about' or 'only ignorant people believe that' will leave you speechless or frantically searching for your nearest blunt instrument.

There's plenty to admire in Dragons, and they always have a long list of fans. Their strength, for instance, is formidable. This can include their strength of mind, because once a Dragon has a goal in sight they'll move heaven and earth to achieve it – and they'll succeed. Their strength of character is stunning – they have a natural authority that always gets them noticed. And their physical strength is legendary. It enables them to keep going when other people are flagging, and it promises a long life. Unfortunately, this strength can also make Dragons less than sympathetic towards other people's aches and pains.

Dragons seem impervious to the effect they have on other people. And such is their charisma and magnetic attraction that the rest of us are usually prepared to forgive a Dragon whenever they step out of conversational line because we realize that they're only being themselves, and they don't mean any harm by it. We also have a good idea that the Dragon is very insecure and unsure of themselves, and they're simply putting on a good show. If a Dragon's harsh words should ever make you burst into tears, they'll be mortified and will do their utmost to comfort you. Dragons are very sentimental beneath that talkative, dogmatic exterior. They're also very loving and affectionate. So, even though your favourite Dragon may remind you that close contact only spreads germs, give them a hug next time you see them and watch that fire-breathing Dragon turn into one emanating contentment and pleasure.

Each sign does better in some years than in others. Dragons make great progress in Dragon, Monkey and Rat years, but encounter difficulties in Dog, Goat and Ox years.

SNAKE

SNAKES HAVE IT ALL. They're intelligent, have excellent taste and are one of the most attractive signs of the Chinese zodiac. They can't help making the most of themselves, and they adore the effect it has on everyone around them. If you live with a Snake, your own space in the wardrobe is probably steadily being eroded, because they have so many clothes that yours are scrunched into a corner to make space. If you travel with a Snake, don't be shocked at the amount of (immaculate) luggage they will bring with them. They need all those bags because each one is full of the scarves, belts, hats, bags and other expensive accessories the Snake could never be seen in public without. They have an image to maintain, you know!

4 FEBRUARY 1905 – 24 JANUARY 1906
23 JANUARY 1917 – 10 FEBRUARY 1918
10 FEBRUARY 1929 – 29 JANUARY 1930
27 JANUARY 1941 – 14 FEBRUARY 1942
14 FEBRUARY 1953 – 2 FEBRUARY 1954
2 FEBRUARY 1965 – 20 JANUARY 1966
18 FEBRUARY 1977 – 6 FEBRUARY 1978
6 FEBRUARY 1989 – 26 JANUARY 1990
24 JANUARY 2001 – 11 FEBRUARY 2002
10 FEBRUARY 2013 – 29 JANUARY 2014

As you might expect, money is usually an issue for Snakes. They need plenty of it in order to be able to maintain their high living standards but, although they'll happily splash out on extravagant fripperies for themselves, they may begrudge paying the day-to-day expenses.

It's only to be expected that such a dazzlingly attractive, beautifully dressed, brainy and cultivated sign should be deluged with admirers. Snakes attract adoring fans the way honey pots attract bees, and that's where the trouble can start. Although Snakes expect total fidelity from their partners, and become wildly jealous when their suspicions are aroused, they're not always eager or willing to return the compliment. To put it bluntly, they're capable of breathtaking double standards. Some Snakes will make sure their partners are fully occupied looking after the family, and then will happily go off and have a good time without them.

Despite this, Snakes are renowned for their wisdom, which makes them the first people you should turn to whenever you're in need of advice. They'll think carefully before giving you the benefit of their experience, and they'll combine these wise words with compassion.

Snakes are notorious for their indolence. As children, they may not bother with their school work because it simply doesn't interest them. Instead, they'll pour all their energies into the activities they do find engrossing, which could be anything from being a budding rock star (think of the wardrobe potential) to becoming an actor (ditto). Snakes are extremely artistic. When they get older, they need to be dedicated to whatever they do for a living, otherwise they'll quickly become dissatisfied and find it difficult to get out of bed in the mornings. They may also prefer to work alone. For all their considerable charm, Snakes have a strong need to be left to their own devices and can find other people either too distracting or too competitive.

Each sign does better in some years than in others. Snakes prosper in Snake, Rooster and Ox years, but don't have such a good time in Pig, Monkey and Tiger years.

HORSE

ORSES NEED TO RUN FREE. They loathe the idea of being tethered by other people's expectations or, for that matter, their opinions, because Horses are, essentially, rebellious. They also have an inner conviction that they're right and everyone else has got it horribly wrong. This can make it very difficult for them to appreciate anyone else's point of view.

One of the biggest Horse pleasures is travelling. While some signs will prefer to spend the journey with their noses stuck in a book or with a pair of headphones clamped to their ears, Horses like to turn to their neighbour and strike up a conversation. You'd be amazed at the intimate information a Horse can entice out of a complete stranger.

25 JANUARY 1906 – 12 FEBRUARY 1907
11 FEBRUARY 1918 – 31 JANUARY 1919
30 JANUARY 1930 – 16 FEBRUARY 1931
15 FEBRUARY 1942 – 4 FEBRUARY 1943
3 FEBRUARY 1954 – 23 JANUARY 1955
21 JANUARY 1966 – 8 FEBRUARY 1967
7 FEBRUARY 1978 – 27 JANUARY 1979
27 JANUARY 1990– 14 FEBRUARY 1991
12 FEBRUARY 2002 – 31 JANUARY 2003
30 JANUARY 2014 – 18 FEBRUARY 2015

Conversation and Horses were made for each other. Horses just love to chat. They particularly enjoy chatting on the phone, and will ignore the size of the bill they're notching up. They really can't be bothered with such piffling trifles as remembering to call long-distance during the cheap-rate periods. If they want to talk to you, then that's what they'll do. Right this minute! Some Horses are so impetuous that this desire for a conversation overrides such considerations as the fact that you might be sound asleep at the time. If you pick up the phone and groggily mumble 'Whazzamarrer? It's three in the morning!' the Horse will blithely reply, 'Is it? I was painting and lost track of the time. Now listen.

Do you think I should decorate my bedroom in green or pink?' It's a testament to their charm that Horses have so many friends who are prepared to put up with such treatment.

Horses can't bear the idea of wasting time. They're such industrious, practical creatures that they have to fill up every minute of the day, and if they're forced into idleness on doctor's orders it'll be enough to make them ill, regardless of what is already wrong with them. Housework and similarly dreary tasks leave Horses cold, and they will scrape together enough cash to pay someone else to do these jobs, even if that means they have to economize by eating nothing but potatoes every Friday. If it gets them out of doing the dusting, so be it.

These lively Horses have many friends and are extremely popular. You never know what they'll do next, although you have to be prepared to do things on their terms. They're interested in all sorts of pursuits, especially if these bring out the innate Horse creativity and dexterity. And if any sign knows how to throw a party, it's a Horse. A Horse party is an event that people will still be talking about years later. Horses are excellent guests, too, because they throw themselves into the proceedings with gusto and enthusiasm.

Each sign does better in some years than in others. Horses gallop through Horse, Tiger and Dog years, but will slow to a trot in Rat, Rabbit and Rooster years.

no!

GOAT

THE GENTLE-HEARTED GOAT needs looking after. These vulnerable creatures have such tender feelings that they arouse your most protective instincts, although it's highly likely that they're feeling the same way about you. That's because they're very sensitive and kind, with a finely tuned ear for a sob story or tale of woe. But don't get the idea they're ghouls or suffer from *schadenfreude*. Far from it – they truly hate to think that the people they care about are feeling miserable or are having a bad time.

You have to be careful when pouring your heart out to a Goat. They're so sympathetic and considerate that there is a danger of dumping all your worries on to them, so you walk away feeling a whole lot better and the Goat is left chewing their fingernails and fearing the worst. And not only on your behalf, but because you've stirred up all sorts of traumas that were lurking in their subconscious. Mind you, they've already got a head-start when it comes to worrying, because these creatures would scoop all the medals going if fretting were to be made an Olympic event. They can also be appallingly pessimistic.

Love is an important ingredient in any Goat's life. Goats have a deep need to belong to someone, and will create their own ready-made family around them if the real thing isn't available for some reason. They also set a great deal of store by their loved ones, and can feel more comfortable living vicariously than getting too involved themselves. Mention your new fad to your Goat friend and they'll probably ring you a few days later absolutely raving about it. Take it as a compliment, because they believe that if this new enthusiasm is good enough for you then it's certainly good enough for them. Besides, it might draw the two of you even closer together, and that's something they'll enjoy very much.

Goats are renowned for their unconventional natures, good taste and creativity. They can pluck ideas out of the air and some of them have made a fortune out of doing so. Nevertheless, most of them prefer to be followers rather than leaders, although they won't take kindly to being bossed about. Well, not too much, anyway. They prefer to feel they're in an equal partnership.

13 FEBRUARY 1907 – 1 FEBRUARY 1908
1 FEBRUARY 1919 – 19 FEBRUARY 1920
17 FEBRUARY 1931 – 5 FEBRUARY 1932
5 FEBRUARY 1943 – 24 JANUARY 1944
24 JANUARY 1955 – 11 FEBRUARY 1956
9 FEBRUARY 1979 – 15 FEBRUARY 1980
15 FEBRUARY 1991 – 3 FEBRUARY 1992
1 FEBRUARY 2003 – 20 JANUARY 2004
19 FEBRUARY 2015 – 7 FEBRUARY 2016

Something Goats can't abide is being hurried or chivvied, because they like to work at their own pace. They need to allow for those days when they won't want to do anything much, and those occasions when keeping their brains on the straight and narrow will be almost impossible because they'll keep straying off into mental byways. Another problem for Goats is punctuality. They are notoriously bad time-keepers, so they do best in careers where they can be left to their own devices.

Each sign does better in some years than in others. Goats frisk about in Goat, Rabbit and Pig years, but will feel tethered in Ox, Dragon and Dog years.

MONKEY

Monkeys are the great fixers of the Chinese zodiac. If you've got a problem that needs sorting out, you'd be wise to take it to the nearest Monkey and let them do the honours for you. They'll gladly get to the bottom of what's wrong and come up with a workable solution that will keep everyone happy. In fact, Monkeys are so skilled in trouble-shooting that many of them turn this useful ability into a fully-fledged career, and find that their services are in great demand. Monkeys like to have something to work towards and will always find a way forward, especially if that involves their innate ability to conduct negotiations and strike deals. However, it

2 February 1908 – 21 January 1909
20 February 1920 – 7 February 1921
6 February 1932 – 25 January 1933
25 January 1944 – 12 February 1945
12 February 1956 – 30 January 1957
30 January 1968 – 16 February 1969
16 February 1980 – 4 February 1981
4 February 1992 – 22 January 1993
21 January 2004 – 8 February 2005
8 February 2016 – 27 January 2017

has to be said that not even they can work miracles all the time, and sometimes they'll have to give up in despair and admit defeat.

A Monkey's emotions tend to veer dramatically between happiness and dejection, and they can become quite restless when things jog along in a steady rut. They need the ups and downs to feel properly alive, which is why they're not the most faithful of creatures. It's not unknown for Monkeys to marry more than once, because their roving eyes and penchant for novelty mean that the grass is always greener on the other side of the restaurant table. If a Monkey's partner wants to keep them on the emotional straight and narrow, they should ensure that life never becomes boring or predictable. They need to inject a little fantasy into their relationship, which will work wonders.

Monkeys are often accused of not being entirely honest, and that's putting it politely. However, before you begin to look askance at the Monkeys in your life and decide you'd better lock up the silver whenever they visit you, let's put things in perspective. Monkeys are skilled negotiators in all areas of life and, as they'll be the first to tell you, you can't negotiate properly by being scrupulously honest. You have to dissemble sometimes, rewrite history or plant an idea in someone's head. However, most Monkeys stop at this and would never dream of doing anything that might attract the forces of law and order. It's a rare Monkey who stoops to crime but, when they do, it'll take nothing less than another Monkey to catch them.

Appearances matter to Monkeys, who spend a lot of time making sure they look good. Some of them can be vain and egotistical, although most simply take pride in their appearance. Not that most of us care what our favourite Monkeys look like, because they're so lovable, life-enhancing and witty that it's always a pleasure to see them whether they're dressed in the latest offerings from Yves St Laurent or an old bin-liner.

Each sign does better in some years than in others. Monkeys jump about in Monkey, Rat and Dragon years, but feel lacklustre in Tiger, Snake and Pig years.

8 9 10
16 18 20
24 27 30

申

ROOSTER

THERE'S ALWAYS ONE astrological sign that manages to collect every brickbat going, and in the Chinese menagerie that sign is the Rooster.

Roosters are sorely misunderstood. Their perfectionist streak, combined with their candour, is often misconstrued as pedantry or harsh criticism, and it would help if they thought for a few seconds before opening their mouths. For a start, it might prevent them saying things that sound honest to them but which carry a sting in the tail for everyone else. And they might realize that not everyone has their own super-high standards.

Not that it would make any difference, because you can't stop a Rooster being a Rooster. Let's say a Rooster rings up for one of their rapid, round-the-houses conversations. They'll comment that you sound nasal and you'll admit you've got a cold. Well, have a pencil ready because the Rooster will immediately start to reel off a list of all the medicines and potions you should take, possibly even getting quite huffy when you insist, mid-sneeze, that you're happy as you are.

Some people see this as an example of typical Rooster bossiness, but it's meant very kindly. Roosters enjoy helping other people and they have so many wide-ranging interests that they're bound to know a little about almost everything. It's just that they can't resist passing on this information, including what's best for your cold.

22 JANUARY 1909 – 9 FEBRUARY 1910
8 FEBRUARY 1921 – 27 JANUARY 1922
26 JANUARY 1933 – 13 FEBRUARY 1934
13 FEBRUARY 1945 – 1 FEBRUARY 1946
31 JANUARY 1957 – 17 FEBRUARY 1958
17 FEBRUARY 1969 – 5 FEBRUARY 1970
5 FEBRUARY 1981 – 24 JANUARY 1982
23 JANUARY 1993 – 9 FEBRUARY 1994
9 FEBRUARY 2005 – 28 JANUARY 2006
28 JANUARY 2017 – 14 FEBRUARY 2018

Roosters can get completely carried away by their latest whim and, if you ask them about it, you'll certainly get a comprehensive answer. You may even privately think that it sounds more like a lecture, and that's another clue to the true Rooster character. Roosters are born teachers. They take enormous pleasure in imparting knowledge, and their shelves are usually groaning with books on their favourite topics. What's more, these interests cover a vast range of diverse subjects, from the esoteric to the traditional, from the practical to the wildest flights of fancy. Roosters enjoy novelty and variety, which is why they're so versatile. They're also multi-talented, and can turn their hands to all kinds of occupations. And they revel in being in the spotlight.

In fact, this can be their saving grace, because life has a habit of dragging Roosters through the peaks and troughs like no other sign. Their star can soar to giddy heights, but sometimes it will plummet down into the depths. Whatever vagaries of life they have to endure, Roosters do it magnificently. They simply pick themselves up and start again. They certainly can't spare the time for remorse or regret at what's happened because they've already hatched up this fantastic new scheme.

Each sign does better in some years than in others. Roosters crow their heads off in Rooster, Ox and Snake years, but their spirits are dampened in Rabbit, Horse and Rat years.

DOG

It's a moot point why some Chinese signs have been given their names, but there's no problem when it comes to Dogs. Like their canine counterparts, Dogs are our best friends. Their loyalty and deep affection remind us of dogs who greet us ecstatically whenever we come home, because these members of the Chinese menagerie are our devoted and staunch supporters. When you have a Dog as a friend, you're rich indeed.

Dogs are the watch-dogs of the zodiac. Give them even the faintest whiff of a miscarriage of justice, and they'll leap onto their hindlegs and start barking. Out will come the pencil and paper, or on will go the computer, and the Dog will be off on a favourite pursuit – fighting on behalf of the underdog. (See how Dogs fit their name so perfectly?) Dogs are tireless champions of good causes, and will happily become embroiled in yet another crusade if they think it will further the cause of justice. It's rare not to find more than the average number of Dogs standing on picket lines, handing out leaflets on street corners, delivering petitions to government offices and writing impassioned letters to the newspapers.

Although Dogs are excellent at defending everyone's rights and ensuring that a sense of fair play is restored, they're not so hot when it comes to watching what's going on in their own back-yards. While they're at the front door haranguing their local politician for their dilatory handling of the latest community scandal, a thief is sneaking in through the back door on the hunt for the Dog's valuables. The same thing happens over money issues and career matters – they're so busy being angry on your behalf and trying to help you to solve your difficulties that they neglect their own problems entirely, and only remember them when it's too late. They're truly selfless, but this can sometimes cause enormous difficulties and setbacks.

Dogs are extremely sensitive and vulnerable creatures. When they're in the company of lively and go-getting friends, they're lively and go-getting too. But when they're surrounded by people who are feeling miserable or who are moaning, the Dog will become gloomy and depressed. Yet it's curious that they can sometimes be so ignorant of the effect they have on other people. Dogs can utter comments that are real zingers, the sort of remark that pins you to your chair and leaves you in shock. Dogs don't mean to offend (not often, anyway); they simply don't realize that what they meant as a joke sounds like a terrible insult to you. All the same, they won't like it if you give as good as you get. Yet Dogs are so loving and affectionate that this isn't a problem which you'll have to face very often.

Each sign does better in some years than in others. Dogs gambol through Dog, Horse and Tiger years, but feel constrained in Dragon, Ox and Goat years.

10 FEBRUARY 1910 – 29 JANUARY 1911
28 JANUARY 1922 – 15 FEBRUARY 1923
14 FEBRUARY 1934 – 3 FEBRUARY 1935
2 FEBRUARY 1946 – 21 JANUARY 1947
18 FEBRUARY 1958 – 7 FEBRUARY 1959
6 FEBRUARY 1970 – 26 JANUARY 1971
25 JANUARY 1982 – 12 FEBRUARY 1983
10 FEBRUARY 1994 – 30 JANUARY 1995
29 JANUARY 2006 – 16 FEBRUARY 2007
15 FEBRUARY 2018 – 4 FEBRUARY 2019

PIG

IKE OSCAR WILDE, Pigs can resist every-thing except temptation. And, for them, temptation comes in many forms. For a start, it often arrives in the shape of boxes of delectable chocolates, sugary Danish pastries, buttery scones, rich fruit cakes … and anything else that lives in the fridge, dwells in the larder or sits in the wine-rack. Pigs and food enjoy one of those unbreakable relation-ships that will warm the heart of every self-respecting member of this sign. If a Pig wakes up hungry in the mid-dle of the night, they think nothing of pad-ding into the kitchen in search of a little some-thing. Unfortunately the tell-tale signs may be more than obvious – as the years go by, there's more and more of the Pig to love, and they're bemused by the way their clothes can shrink in the wardrobe.

30 JANUARY 1911 – 17 FEBRUARY 1912
16 FEBRUARY 1923 – 4 FEBRUARY 1924
4 FEBRUARY 1935 – 23 JANUARY 1936
22 JANUARY 1947 – 9 FEBRUARY 1948
8 FEBRUARY 1959 – 27 JANUARY 1960
27 JANUARY 1971 – 14 FEBRUARY 1972
13 FEBRUARY 1983 – 1 FEBRUARY 1984
31 JANUARY 1995 – 18 FEBRUARY 1996
17 FEBRUARY 2007 – 6 FEBRUARY 2008
23 JANUARY 2012 – 9 FEBRUARY 2013

Food offers tremendous comfort to Pigs. They are so emotionally vulnerable that they're prey to every unscrupulous hustler and self-serving low-life for miles around. Pigs just can't say 'no'. If you want to ask someone a favour and be sure of having it granted, cast your eye around for the nearest Pig. If it's humanly possible, they'll accede to your wishes. True, they may occasionally wonder why they're doing so, especially if they suspect that you're perfectly capable of perform-ing the task yourself, but do it they will. That's why it's so easy to take advantage of a Pig, should you be base enough to want to try – Pigs are so gullible. It's also why they have their hearts broken so often by lovers who fail to appreciate them fully. However, don't think you can save them from themselves by giving them the occa-sional word of advice, perhaps about putting themselves first for a change. The Pig will listen pensively, then greet every suggestion with 'Yes, but …'. It's almost as if they want to suffer.

Another temptation that's difficult for Pigs to resist is the ability to pretend that every-thing's hunkydory when it so obviously isn't. Pigs staring disaster or ruin in the face will reso-lutely insist that this is simply a glitch, and tell you that they're reluc-tant to dip into their rainy-day fund because they're keeping that for emergencies. They hate to deal with unpleasant facts or unpalatable truths, and will blithely carry on as if nothing's wrong for as long as possible. Mind you, even Pigs can reach breaking point eventually, and that's quite a frightening sight. After months, or even years, of being put upon and taken for granted, they'll finally snap.

The one temptation that leaves Pigs cold is dis-honesty. Pigs have hearts of gold. They flourish in close relationships and need partners who'll treat them properly and love them in the way that they deserve.

Each sign does better in some years than in others. Pigs are in clover in Pig, Goat and Rabbit years, but have to forage around in Snake, Tiger and Monkey years.

COMPATIBILITY IN LOVE AND SEX

WOMAN MAN	RAT	OX	TIGER	RABBIT	DRAGON	SNAKE
RAT	You were made for each other!	Highly enjoyable	You have little in common	Rows galore!	Heaven on earth	Not an easy encounter
OX	Fantastic!	Cosy, safe and happy	Ox is too serious for Tiger	Ox will wear the trousers	You've got your work cut out	You share the same aims
TIGER	A lot of hard work	Not an easy pairing	You're too similar for comfort	Rabbit could get hurt	Highly colourful	Prepare for rows!
RABBIT	Rat will bully Rabbit	Good fun	Tiger will run rings round Rabbit	You'll help each other	Too lively for Rabbit	Snake will coax Rabbit to have fun
DRAGON	You're good for each other	Tricky to say the least	A fearless duo	Lighten up, Dragon!	You've met your match!	You're great friends
SNAKE	Decide who's boss!	Blissful!	Oil and water	Let your hair down, Rabbit!	A proud and feisty pair	Very expensive!
HORSE	An uphill struggle	Horse will lead Ox by the nose	Sexy, sensual and fun	All a bit difficult	Great fun	Not an easy couple
GOAT	Awkward and painful	You view life in different ways	Difficult	A gentle couple	Good as friends	Not very exciting
MONKEY	A laugh a minute	Very difficult	A very lively pair	Great if you compromise	A great team	Dicey
ROOSTER	Proceed with caution	Satisfaction guaranteed!	At emotional odds	Either great or ghastly	Noisy and enjoyable	Enormous fun
DOG	Easy-going and relaxing	Cuddly and warm	Ten out of ten!	You'll protect each other	Nothing in common	Snake could hurt Dog
PIG	Good if Rat can be gentle	You'll jog along	Could do better	Very peaceful	Pig is too sensitive	The potential for trouble
MAN WOMAN	RAT	OX	TIGER	RABBIT	DRAGON	SNAKE

HORSE	GOAT	MONKEY	ROOSTER	DOG	PIG	WOMAN / MAN
Are you sure about this?	You're too different	Lively and good fun	A big clash of egos	Great stuff!	A very sensual pair	RAT
Has the potential for pain	What do you have in common?	Chalk and cheese	Too good to be true!	You'll rely on each other	Not very exciting	OX
Wow! Hot stuff!	Short but not very sweet	Monkey will keep Tiger on their toes	Not a good idea	The perfect couple	Take care, Pig!	TIGER
Not an easy couple	Home-loving and happy	You'll dream and scheme together	You fence around each other	Happy ever after!	A gentle pairing	RABBIT
Terrific!	Lacking in passion	Magnificent!	Lively debates and good fun	Awkward	Pig could feel crushed	DRAGON
A recipe for disaster	OK but not great	Little in common	Fantastic!	Seven out of ten	You're too different	SNAKE
Very sensual	You're good for each other	Horse will get hurt	Lively and good fun	Good for both of you	An enduring pair	HORSE
Entertaining	Partners for life	A good team	You don't understand each other	Dog is too strong for Goat	Made for each other!	GOAT
Play fair, Monkey!	Plenty of fun	You egg each other on	Very good indeed	Plenty of effort needed	You help each other	MONKEY
You'll chat all day	Little in common	Great for you both	Ego clashes are likely	You're too different	Not bad at all	ROOSTER
Not bad at all	A lot of hard work	Tricky	Needs a lot of effort	Home-loving and happy	Comfy and cosy	DOG
Watch out, Pig!	Happiness all the way	Mutually beneficial	Good for you both	Easy-going	Deep understanding	PIG
HORSE	GOAT	MONKEY	ROOSTER	DOG	PIG	MAN / WOMAN

COMPATIBILITY IN BUSINESS

WOMAN ⟍ MAN	RAT	OX	TIGER	RABBIT	DRAGON	SNAKE
RAT	Dynamic	Great if Ox holds the fort	Heavy-going	Difficult	What a team!	Good fun
OX	Divide the work up evenly	Don't work too hard!	You rub each other up the wrong way	Great!	Sparks will fly	Terrific!
TIGER	Feisty	Chalk and cheese	A money-making team	Not very exciting	Fantastic!	You're too different
RABBIT	Tricky for Rabbit	Enjoyable	Awkward	Excellent!	Dragon will be the boss	Rabbit will learn a lot
DRAGON	Aim high!	Awkward	A great team	Success is yours	Noisy!	Easy-going
SNAKE	You'll enjoy yourselves	You'll have fun	Prepare for rows	Great stuff!	Amiable	Powerful!
HORSE	Hard work	Not easy	Lively but tense	Difficult	Two high-fliers	Could go far
GOAT	Too much for Goat	Little in common	Short-term only	You can't fail	A happy pair	Easy does it!
MONKEY	You can't fail!	Oil and water	Tiger is too honest	Do you understand each other?	A great team	Not an easy couple
ROOSTER	Ego clashes	Not bad at all!	Not much in common	Awkward	A very lively couple	Enjoyable
DOG	A great team	Excellent!	Dicey	You'll both enjoy this	Dog will suffer	Agree to disagree
PIG	You share the same goals	Not good, not bad	Not easy	A strong team	Highly profitable	Awkward
MAN ⟍ WOMAN	RAT	OX	TIGER	RABBIT	DRAGON	SNAKE

HORSE	GOAT	MONKEY	ROOSTER	DOG	PIG	WOMAN / MAN
Power clashes	Not a happy pair	The perfect couple	You both know best!	Excellent	Brilliant!	RAT
Difficult	Tricky	Monkey is too wily	A hard-working team	Perfect!	All a bit flat	OX
Ego clashes	Won't last long	Your morals differ	Expect rows	Very difficult	Pig could regret this	TIGER
A lot of effort needed	Terrific!	Not easy	Ego clashes	Good friends	A money-making team	RABBIT
Very powerful	Very good indeed	You'll go far	Marvellous	Chalk and cheese	The cash will pour in	DRAGON
Great potential	Love-hate feelings	Snake could suffer	Combine work with chat	Needs give and take	You can't work each other out	SNAKE
Big rewards	Be kind to each other	Dutiful but dull	Stick with it!	Fantastic!	Pig will learn a lot	HORSE
Tough for Goat	The sky's the limit!	Great for both of you	Lots of patience needed	Hard work	A great team	GOAT
Monkey is all at sea	Fantastic!	What a team!	Expect a few rows	You're too different	Surprisingly good	MONKEY
Great in the long term	Take it one step at a time	Be patient with each other	Which one's boss?	Diligent and profitable	Very good indeed	ROOSTER
Exciting and successful	A struggle	Not easy at all	You'll go far	Loyal and devoted	You have a lot in common	DOG
Very good indeed	Very enjoyable	Good fun for both of you	Entertaining	A good team	Expect to make money!	PIG
HORSE	GOAT	MONKEY	ROOSTER	DOG	PIG	MAN / WOMAN

Palmistry

The study of palmistry is fascinating, and once you know the basics, it's

wonderfully easy to read people's hands. You don't need a pack of cards, you

don't have to ask them their date of birth – you simply need to see their

hands. Palmistry can even be practised in a rather covert way. When

you're attending an interview or important meeting, for instance,

you will be able to learn a lot about the other people from the

shapes of their hands and fingers. Although palmistry can

be extremely complex, this chapter contains enough

information to make you a proficient palmist.

EVERYONE'S HANDS tell a fascinating story and one that is unique to them. The excitement of palmistry lies in being able to trace the events of someone's life, as well as their character traits, through the marks on their palms. Sometimes you'll be able to ask someone if they'd like you to read their palms, but at other times you may find it useful simply to make some quiet observations of your own. For instance, if you meet someone for the first time and you want a clue to their character, you can tell a great deal just by looking at the shape of their hands, the length of their fingers and the colour of their nails, and also how they use their hands. Do they wave them about while making extravagant gestures? Do they bunch up their fingers? Do they make stabbing motions with their index fingers?

Before you read someone's palm, there are only four questions you can reasonably ask – the person's name (this means you can address them by name, which builds up the rapport between you); their age (not essential, but it will give you some idea of whether events shown in the palm have already taken place); whether they are right- or left-handed; and, if you're interested in astrology, their Sun sign (which will give you a general impression of their personality).

HOW TO BEGIN

When you start to read palms, you'll probably feel bemused by so much information. What do you look at first? What do you do if you don't like what you see? How do you start?

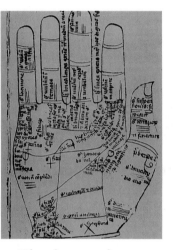

Fifteenth-century diagram

Sit facing the person whose hands you are going to read. It's easiest if you are separated by a table on which the person can rest their hands in case they get tired, but a cushion on your lap would do just as well. Make sure you are sitting in a good light and, if necessary, shine a spotlight or lamp on the person's hands so that you can see all the lines clearly.

Start by asking the person to hold their palms out in front of you. Watch the way they do this, and the pattern their fingers and thumbs make, because it will tell you a lot about their personality. Someone who holds their fingers and thumbs together is reserved and cautious. They may also be mean with money, but you'll need to look for other signs of this before pronouncing judgement. Someone who splays out their fingers and thumbs has an open, generous personality. Look for any big gaps between the fingers even when they are closed (the significance of this is described later). If they hold their little (Mercury) finger apart from the other fingers, it means they always keep a part of themselves private from other people.

Now you're ready to start the reading. If the person is right-handed, this is the hand that describes the events in their life, while the left hand describes what is possible or is wished for. For left-handers, it's the other way around. Work through the hand systematically, which will help to ensure you don't miss any important details. Start by studying the palm's basic shape and

Opposite: French hand-tinted engraving

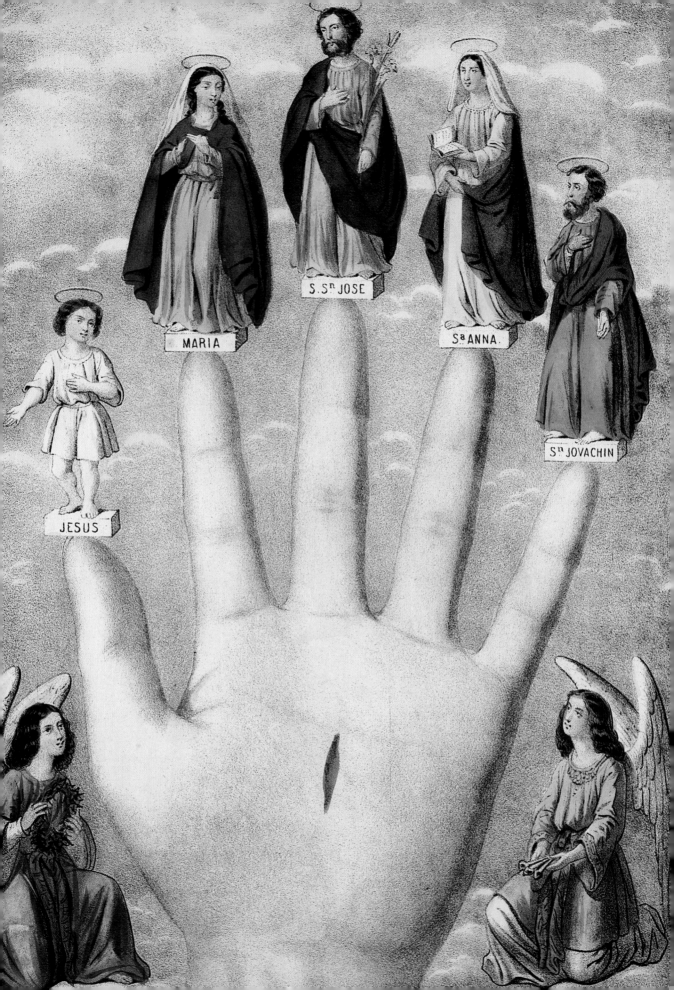

colouring, then look at the lines. Are there a great many or can you only see the major lines? Feel the texture and warmth of the hand. Is it sweaty? Cold? Clammy? Pleasantly warm? Is the hand fleshy, fatty, muscular or bony? Look at the fingers, noting their shape and length. Turn over the fingertips and study the nails. Look at the thumb. By now you'll have begun to form a basic impression of the individual's personality. Next, start to look at the lines.

As you study the person's hands, keep chatting. This not only breaks what could otherwise

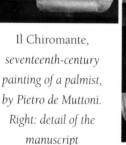

*Il Chiromante,
seventeenth-century
painting of a palmist,
by Pietro de Muttoni.
Right: detail of the
manuscript*

be an uncomfortable silence but also puts both of you at your ease and establishes a rapport between you. You don't have to say very much, especially if you're a beginner, but you should certainly say something. Describe what you are seeing – if someone wants their palm read they'll be fascinated to know what you think of it (everyone believes their palm is remarkable in some

way). Say positive things such as, 'You've got very long fingers, which means that you have a powerful imagination.' Don't say things like 'Oh, you bite your nails!' – instead, think about what bitten nails might indicate and say something like, 'You're very sensitive and are sometimes rather unsure of yourself. I expect that you burn up a lot of emotional energy through worry.'

Describe what you can see, and what it means, but don't blind the person with science. You are their guide to what, you hope, will be fresh insights into their personality, so lead them there gently. As you become a more confident palmist, you'll be able to use your intuition as well, but in the early stages you should simply rely on your palm-reading skills.

One of the best ways to practise palmistry is by studying your own hands. You can scrutinize the lines carefully, using a magnifying glass if necessary, and compare their formation with the character traits described in this chapter. This is one of the most effective ways of remembering the meanings of the different markings and of discovering how they work in your life. Once you know this, you will gain a good understanding of how they might operate in other people's lives. However, be warned that it is not at all easy to be objective about what you see in your own palm: it is human nature to concentrate on the positive traits and markings and to ignore or dismiss the negative ones. If you truly want an objective reading of your own palms, you may have to consult another palmist.

THE HAND

When you first begin to study palmistry, and you're presented with someone's upturned palm, you may wonder where on earth you should begin. For instance, do you pitch straight in with

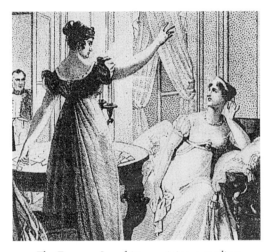

The Empress Josephine receiving a reading

whichever line is most striking? In fact, the best way to read a palm is in the systematic order given in this chapter, starting with the basic shape of the hand. If you always follow this order, you will gain a general insight into the energies that are operating in the person's life, and as a result you will ensure that you don't overlook any important areas of the palm.

THE BASIC SHAPES OF THE HAND

The shape of someone's hand will tell you a great deal about their character. Many experts classify hands into the four basic shapes described by the palmist Fred Gettings, because they show the way the person's energy flows. These classifications are also easy to distinguish and remember, because they are based on whether the palm is fundamentally square or rectangular and whether

the fingers are long or short. The four types are composed of combinations of these shapes. Although their names correspond to the four elements of the zodiac, they are independent of the person's zodiac type – so, for instance, you can be an Earth sign with a Water hand.

Fingers are classified as long if the middle finger is at least three-quarters the length of the palm. If it's shorter than this, the fingers are short. If you're unsure whether a palm is square or rectangular, measure it from the base of the middle finger to the base of the palm, and then from side to side. Be prepared to allow a little leeway in this. For instance, if your measurements reveal that the palm is more square than rectangular, although it is not precisely so, then you should still consider the palm to be square. There is no need for your measurements to be exact.

The Earth Hand

This hand has a square palm and short fingers. The lines are thick and easy to read, with few subsidiary lines, and the skin tends to be thick and coarse. This person is practical, reliable, uncomplicated, matter-of-fact and full of common sense. They are conventional and find it difficult to adapt to change. In relationships, they look for a partner they can trust and who is as steady and forthright as themselves. Unless there are indications to the contrary in the hand, they are healthy and will quickly recover when laid low. People with Earth hands often have jobs that bring them into contact with the earth or that involve hard, physical labour. They prefer being in the country to the town.

The Fire Hand

This hand has a long palm and short fingers, with many strong, clear minor lines in addition to the major ones. The skin is firm and warm. These people are full of energy, which makes them impulsive, daring and feisty. They hate being inactive and are usually energetic, competitive and adventurous. People with Fire hands like to be in control of situations and to influence other people, and they enjoy being the centre of attention. They need careers that draw on these qualities, that allow them to take the lead and that bring them plenty of excitement and mental stimulation. They are usually fit and strong, although they may have a tendency to eat and drink too much. The partner of someone with a Fire hand must be good fun, lively and entertaining, but happy to take a back seat while the Fire person holds the stage.

The Air Hand

This hand has a square palm and long fingers. The lines are strongly marked but may be quite thin, and the skin is dry and soft. Someone with an Air hand is inquisitive and usually intelligent, and enjoys using their brain. Knowledge is very important to them and they strive to find connections between people and places, events and ideas. They are independent and need emotional freedom, even if they don't use it. When looking for a partner, this person will place personality above looks. They may not get married, or become emotionally committed, until relatively late in life, yet they have stable emotions. Communication is very important to them, and they enjoy expressing their ideas. As a result, they may be drawn to a career that enables them to do this, such as the arts, writing, teaching, journalism, public relations or television.

The Water Hand

This hand has a long palm and long fingers, with many fine, subsidiary, vertical lines running across the palm. The major lines may also be fine, and may be braided or chained (ie, resembling links of a chain rather than perfectly straight). The skin is damp and soft. The owner of the Water hand is emotional, sensitive and easily influenced by their surroundings. They are also easily influenced by other people, whether for good or ill, so should be selective about the company they keep – negative people and surroundings may even affect their health. This sensitivity can make them creative, and traditionally people with Water hands have quiet but excellent taste. They're drawn to careers that enable them to express their artistic abilities, such as the beauty business, fashion, modelling or interior design, or occupations which bring out their thoughtful and studious qualities. In relationships, these people look for someone who is kind, sensitive and reliable. Water hands are delicate and often their owners look fragile too, and are usually slim.

PERCUSSION

This is the term given to the shape of the outer side of the palm, and it is visible whether the fingers are open or closed. Does it go straight down or is it curved? A curve indicates someone who is artistic. They may use their own talents or simply appreciate other people's creative gifts. A straight percussion indicates someone who doesn't have artistic talents and who is probably extremely practical instead.

THE FINGERS

In palmistry, each of the fingers is named after a different Roman god. The index finger is named after Jupiter, the middle finger after Saturn, the ring finger after Apollo and the little finger after Mercury. (If you have difficulty recalling all these names at first, just remember the simple acronym 'JSAM', which always starts with the index finger and moves out to the little finger.)

Each finger tells its own story and influences a different set of characteristics. When you look at someone's hand, study each finger in turn and compare their lengths. In a normal hand, the Saturn finger is the longest one, followed by the Jupiter finger which generally reaches the middle of the top section of the Saturn finger, then the Apollo finger which is usually slightly shorter, and finally the Mercury finger which normally reaches the joint of the top phalange of the Apollo finger. In some hands, you'll find that the Mercury finger is set quite low down on the palm, so appears to be very short. This can be deceptive, however, so gently cup the hand until the bases of the Mercury and Apollo fingers are level, and then measure them – the Mercury finger may be longer than you think.

An excellent indication of someone's character is whether they wear any rings and, if so, on which fingers. Ignore wedding rings, unless the person is wearing several of them or you know they've never been married or in a close emotional relationship.

Remember to consider each finger's length in relation to the person's other fingers, so that if they have long or short fingers in general, you allow for this.

THE JUPITER FINGER

This is the index finger. It shows how much pride someone has, and the strength of their need for power. Compare the length of this finger with the other fingers. If the Jupiter finger is short, it signifies someone who prefers to follow rather than lead. They are shy, reserved and lacking in self-esteem and may shrink from challenges and responsibilities. (These qualities will be emphasized if you are looking at a Water hand, or if the rest of the hand shows a very sensitive nature – in which case, choose your words carefully!)

A long Jupiter finger indicates someone who is proud and ambitious, possibly arrogant, and has a strong desire for power – Napoleon's Jupiter fingers, for example, were abnormally long. (To see if the person has the determination and willpower to realize these dreams, also look at the thumb – see page 138.)

Is there a significant gap between the Jupiter and Saturn fingers? If so, the person is a good manager and is able to take decisions and use their initiative; it's a good sign for someone who wants to become self-employed. If the finger juts out, it indicates someone who's an exhibitionist and likes to be the centre of attention.

A person who wears a ring on this finger (and it's often a huge, couldn't-miss-it-with-your-eyes-closed ring) wants to boost their confidence. They wish to appear powerful, although they may feel the opposite. If the finger is short, this is

especially true. If it's long and prominent, the person may have an enormous ego – as, no doubt, you'll soon discover.

The straighter the Jupiter finger, the keener the person's powers of observation will be, both figuratively and literally – people with straight Jupiter fingers rarely need to wear glasses. If the finger curves towards the middle finger, this means that the person is acquisitive and is cautious when dealing with others.

THE SATURN FINGER

This is the middle finger. It indicates a person's general character and also their sense of responsibility. Most people have Saturn fingers measuring about three-quarters of the length of the palm. They have a balanced nature and are able to shoulder their fair share of responsibility without feeling cowed or becoming careless.

Someone with a long Saturn finger has a strong character, is reliable and dependable, and takes life seriously. Successful business people, particularly those who handle other people's money, usually have long Saturn fingers. If the finger is long and also very chunky, the person makes heavy weather of life and may suffer from depression. (These traits are especially emphasized if the head line takes a nosedive into the mount of Luna – see page 141.)

A short Saturn finger indicates someone who makes impulsive decisions and avoids taking responsibility. If it's very short, this person may be unable to make commitments involving marriage, owning property and so on.

It's unusual for people to wear rings on their Saturn fingers. When they do, it shows that they want to boost their sense of security. They may have a troubled family background, an important relationship may have just ended or their life may be going through many changes.

A straight Saturn finger indicates someone who can balance their need to be sociable with their need to be alone. If it leans towards the Jupiter finger, the person is extrovert and enjoys spending most of their time with other people. If it leans towards the Apollo finger, they need plenty of time to themselves.

THE APOLLO FINGER

This is the ring finger, which is associated with creativity and artistic talents. It's also connected with the emotions, and with the (often unconscious) way in which we communicate with other people. Usually, this finger is shorter than the Jupiter and Saturn fingers. If so, the person is well balanced emotionally.

If it's longer than normal (in other words, longer than the Jupiter finger or almost as long as a normal Saturn finger), it signifies someone who experiences powerful emotions and has no trouble in expressing them. There is often a very strong sex drive. A long Apollo finger also indicates that the person is creative – the general shape of their hand will tell you how this creativity is used. They are good at communicating with others and find it easy to express their ideas and opinions.

A short Apollo finger indicates that the person has trouble in adjusting to other people's emotional demands, and may find it hard to express their own emotions. They may seem slightly apathetic or lacking in energy, and they may not be very creative.

If the Saturn and Apollo fingers bend towards each other, the person has a tendency to sacrifice pleasure for duty. They may have had to put their creative desires second to the need to make money, or perhaps they spend a lot of time looking after their loved ones and have little time or energy left for themselves.

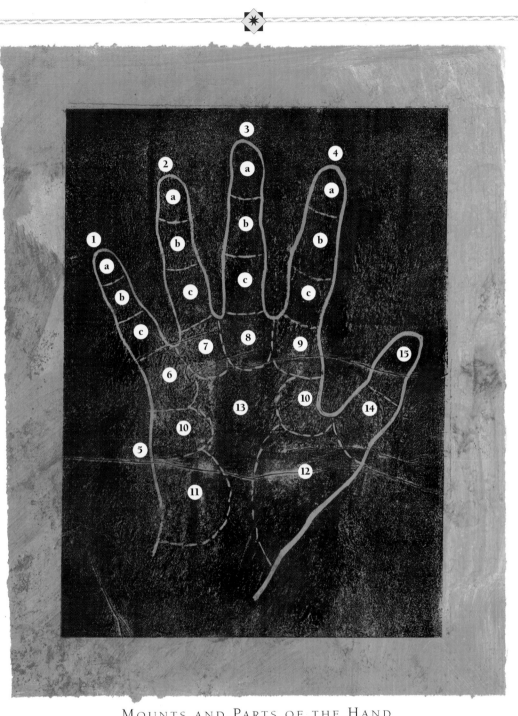

MOUNTS AND PARTS OF THE HAND

1 Mercury Finger

2 Apollo Finger

3 Saturn Finger

4 Jupiter Finger

a Top Phalange

b Middle Phalange

c Base Phalange

5 Percussion

6 Mount of Mercury

7 Mount of Apollo

8 Mount of Saturn

9 Mount of Jupiter

10 Mount of Mars

11 Mount of Luna

12 Mount of Venus

13 Plain of Mars

14 Logic

15 Will

Because the Apollo finger is the ring finger, a ring on this finger doesn't usually have any special significance unless there's something very striking about the ring or unless the person is wearing several rings on that finger. If so, they are trying to compensate for what they feel is a lack of creativity or a lack of love in their lives. Be careful how you phrase this!

THE MERCURY FINGER

This is the little finger. Take care when measuring the length of the Mercury finger against the other fingers on the hand. As already mentioned, a Mercury finger may look very short because it's set low down on the palm, but when you measure it against the other fingers you may discover it's actually quite long. This finger rules communication so you can safely assume that the longer it is, the better the person is able to communicate with others.

Not only does a long Mercury finger denote the ability to communicate well, but it also signifies considerable intelligence (which will be backed up by a strong, clearly marked head line). This person is sociable and gets on well with others. They may also be lively and talkative.

A short Mercury finger indicates someone who has problems in communicating. They may behave in a childlike, immature way and find it difficult to form close emotional relationships.

If there's a notable gap between the Mercury and Apollo fingers when the fingers are closed, the person finds it difficult to communicate with others on an emotional level. Even if the Mercury finger is long, which indicates that they are chatty and talkative, they will find it hard to draw closer to others. If the finger seems to be separate from the rest of the hand, almost as if it's been stuck on as an afterthought, it indicates someone who is unconventional, original and independent. They

Portrait of the German chiromant (palmist) Johann Hartlieb, whose book Die Kunst Ciromantia *was published in 1448*

may also find it difficult to reveal some aspects of their lives to other people.

If you ever meet someone that you instinctively distrust, sneak a look at their Mercury fingers. The straighter they are, the more honest the person is. If one or both fingers shows a slight leaning towards the Apollo finger, the person is shrewd, astute and possibly successful in business. But a naturally curved or bent Mercury finger (ignore fingers that have been twisted through accidents or arthritis) indicates someone who doesn't mind bending the truth when it suits them. Rings worn on this finger signify the desire for sexual independence.

THE PHALANGES OF THE FINGERS

Most people have three sections, or phalanges, to their fingers – the top, middle and base. The size and fleshiness of the phalanges will give you further clues about someone's personality. Incidentally, the fleshiness of someone's fingers may have little connection with their weight – slim people can have fat hands, while overweight people may have very delicate fingers.

THE BASE PHALANGES

Look at the base phalanges. Are they puffy, fleshy or thin? Fleshy base phalanges indicate someone who is sensual, and who enjoys material comforts and luxuries. They may be acquisitive or materialistic, and not very generous. Someone with thin base phalanges is intellectual and may even seem slightly detached from everyday worries, with their mind dwelling on matters they find more important. If there are notable gaps between the base of each finger, the person is generous and may spend virtually every penny they earn.

THE JOINTS

The joints of a person's fingers tell you a lot about the way their mind works. (Ignore any bumps or deformed joints caused by arthritis or bone complaints, as these will be misleading.)

People with very smooth fingers, with no noticeable bumps at the joints, tend to rely on their instincts when making decisions. They jump to conclusions, which may or may not be accurate, without reasoning things out. Longer fingers help to offset this. If the fingers are short, the person is particularly impulsive, especially if they also have a weak head line.

Knotty joints indicate someone who is philosophical, and who enjoys puzzling out the whys and wherefores of meaty problems. They will reason and analyse, and they will always pay close attention to detail.

THE FINGERTIPS

Turn the hand over and study the fingertips. Look for droplets, which are little raised pads of flesh, indicating artistic talents and a strong sensitivity towards the surroundings. This person feels things very deeply and may also be psychic. If the fingertips are firm, the person is good at business. They don't like being told what to do and they adopt a no-nonsense approach to life.

THE NAILS

The shape of the nails offers further clues about someone's personality. An average nail is half the length of the top phalange of the finger or thumb. In general, long nails denote a dreamer – someone who is artistic and imaginative; they may shy away from unpleasant facts. Short nails belong to someone who's sceptical, logical, critical of others and has a short temper. If the nails are broader than they are long, the person is argumentative, worries a lot and is easily offended. If the nails are very narrow, the person is narrow-minded and dogmatic.

If they're bitten, the person is highly strung and nervy. If the nails are beautifully manicured, then obviously this is someone who sets great store by appearance. White flecks on the nails indicate shocks to the nervous system – the area of life ruled by the finger involved will tell you what these shocks are likely to have entailed. Visible half-moons show that the person breathes properly (most people take rather shallow breaths) and takes lots of exercise. The reverse is true if the half-moons aren't visible. Very large half-moons may indicate heart trouble.

THE THUMB

This is one of the most important elements of someone's hand, because it indicates their amount of willpower, the way their energies flow, their mental abilities and the strength of their character. Essentially, the weaker the thumb, the weaker the person's mind and personality; and the stronger the thumb is, the more domineering and powerful the person.

First, look at the position of the thumb on the hand. Is it set very high or low on the hand, or roughly halfway down? A very high thumb, near the Jupiter (index) finger, denotes someone who's opinionated and has a pronounced ego. A thumb set halfway down the hand is normal, indicating someone with an average ego, neither too pronounced nor too muted. A low-set thumb indicates a possible lack of intellect. This person is practical, with little imagination.

Now check the angle that's formed between the thumb and the hand when you gently pull the thumb downwards. The closer the thumb sits to the hand, the more cautious the person. They may also be easily swayed by other people's arguments. The wider the angle, the more generous and impulsive they are. If the thumb creates an angle over 90 degrees, the person is hot-tempered and a real nonconformist. They want to go their own way and won't listen to anyone who tries to persuade them otherwise. If the thumb on the hand used most often has a smaller angle than the other thumb, the person would like to be more spontaneous but finds this difficult.

Next, study the length of the thumb. The average thumb is the same length as the Mercury (little) finger and, when held against the hand, should reach somewhere between the base and middle phalanges of the Jupiter finger. A long Mercury finger therefore denotes a long thumb. A thumb of average length indicates someone who's able to combine assertiveness with appreciation of others and sensitivity towards them. Someone with a long thumb is assertive, is in control of their surroundings and has a strong character. If the thumb is also broad, this person knows what they want from life and they usually get it. If the thumb is long but narrow, the person still knows what they want from life but may not have enough driving force to achieve it. A long, well-developed thumb indicates someone with good mental abilities, who's able to use reason in arguments and has plenty of willpower.

A short thumb indicates someone with a weak character. They may be a day-dreamer or reluctant to think for themselves, preferring to be told what to do. If the thumb is broad but short, the person has plenty of energy but they find it difficult to motivate themselves. If it's short and narrow, the person is emotionally flighty and weak-willed, and will drift through life. A puny, poorly shaped thumb signifies someone weak, easily bullied and lacking in energy and who has few opinions of their own.

Now compare the length of the two phalanges of the thumb. The top one denotes will, and the lower one logic. Therefore, a longer top phalange indicates someone whose head rules their heart – they're impulsive and want to get their own way, no matter what. If this phalange is also broad and bulbous, the person is a bully who is obstinate and relies on brute force to get what they want; if, in addition, the whole thumb is short, they may be violent. A longer second phalange indicates someone who is logical and who reasons things out before taking action. If this phalange is

Opposite: title page of
Ludiclrum Chriomanticum Praetoris, *showing how to read palms and faces.*

exceptionally long, the person may do a lot of thinking but rarely take any action at all. This phalange is often waisted (thinner at the centre), which indicates someone who uses tact and diplomacy when trying to get their own way. If this 'waist' is very pronounced, the person tends to be logical to a fault, is easily influenced by other people's cogent arguments and may endlessly analyse their own actions.

Look at the top phalange from the side. If it's flat and thin, the person is highly strung and sensitive. If it's rounded and fleshy, they are blunt and uncomfortably forthright. If it's abnormally large, the person is obstinate and may be violent.

Finally, test the flexibility of the thumb. Does the top phalange bend backwards? If it bends a short way it denotes someone who's adaptable and versatile, although this may make them unreliable and changeable at times. If the thumb is virtually double-jointed, the person sometimes has a flimsy grasp of the truth, changing it to suit their needs. If the thumb is very rigid and won't move at all, this suggests that the person is reliable, practical and steadfast, although they may be resistant to change.

THE MOUNTS

These are the small, fleshy pads that appear on the palm. In some hands the mounts are pronounced while in others only a few mounts are visible, or they look as if they've been squashed. To see the mounts most clearly, cup the hand very slightly. In general, the more pronounced the mounts are, the more lively and enthusiastic that person is; their life is very full. If the mounts are almost non-existent, the person just jogs along in life and never gets very excited about anything. They may be rather listless, lacking vitality and physical stamina.

MOUNTS BENEATH THE FINGERS

Each finger has its own mount, which appears beneath it on the palm. Very often, a mount does not appear directly beneath the fingers but between them. If so, interpret it by combining the meanings of the two mounts involved, such as the Jupiter and Saturn mounts.

The Mount of Jupiter

A well-shaped mount of Jupiter, which sits at the base of the index, or Jupiter, finger, indicates ambition and the desire for success. These are taken to extremes if the mount is over-large. If the life line is strong and clearly marked, this person's ambitions will be realized, but if it is weak and meandering, the person never achieves very much and yet feels proud and self-satisfied. An over-developed mount, coupled with a large mount of Mars beneath it, denotes a bully. A small mount indicates a lack of confidence.

The Mount of Saturn

If the mount of Saturn, at the base of the middle finger, is non-existent, the person takes a frivolous view of life. Before reaching this conclusion, however, check that the mount hasn't merged with one of its neighbours, in which case it will blend a practical nature with ambition (Jupiter) or artistic talents (Apollo). If it's very pronounced, the person is studious and serious; they may also be pessimistic or fatalistic. A well-shaped mount of Saturn indicates someone who enjoys solitude and is a hard worker.

The Mount of Apollo

This mount, at the base of the ring finger, is an excellent one to have. When it's well shaped, it indicates creative talents and a love of beauty. The person is generous and expansive. If it's very large, this is someone who enjoys being in the limelight and may be a show-off. A small or non-existent mount of Apollo indicates lack of artistic ability.

The Mount of Mercury

Sitting below the little finger, this mount is always considered in relation to the rest of the hand, and especially the head line, because it amplifies existing tendencies. If the rest of the hand is positive and the head line is long and also clearly marked, this is a most favourable mount show- ing quick thinking, live- liness and wit. If the rest of the hand is negative, and the head line is weak or is badly marked, this mount indicates sarcasm, quick wits that can lead to sharp practice or crime, lack of concentration and an over-excitable nature.

OTHER MOUNTS ON THE HAND

The other mounts that are found on the hand are just as important as those lying beneath the fin- gers. They are frequently easier to see than the finger mounts.

The Mounts of Mars

There are two of these – one is just below the mount of Jupiter and the other below the mount of Mercury.

The one below the mount of Jupiter indicates physical courage. If it's well developed, the person is brave and fearless. They may be prepared to fight physically for what they believe in – many people in the armed services have this mount. However, if the mount is very large the person

may also be dogmatic, foolhardy and impulsive, rushing in where angels fear to tread. If the mount is very small or non-existent, the person lacks physical courage.

The mount of Mars below the mount of Mercury denotes moral courage. When well developed, it shows someone who has spiritual strength, will- power and the ability to follow their beliefs in the face of opposition. If the mount is overdeveloped, however, the person will doggedly and blindly persist in their beliefs, as if they are on a mission to prove something. This may, of course, end in disaster.

The Plain of Mars

This sits in the centre of the palm, surrounded by all the mounts. The best way to exam- ine it is to massage it gently with the ball of your thumb. If the skin is soft and you can feel the person's bones and lig- aments through their skin, they lack self-confi- dence. If the skin is firm and elastic, the person has plenty of confidence and may even be rather bumptious at times. If the skin is coarse and the plain of Mars is very full, this denotes someone who enjoys the sound of their own voice and appears insensitive to other people's feelings.

The Mount of Luna

This mount is found at the outer edge of the hand, below the mount of Mars and just above the wrist. If it's very plump, it suggests someone who is dreamy and idealistic and who lives in a little world of their own. They may have a ten- uous grasp of reality, which could lead to lies or

half-truths – check the Mercury finger and the head line. A well-developed mount indicates someone who is imaginative, artistic and cultured and who may experience ESP (extra-sensory perception). The flatter the mount is, the more realistic the person.

The Mount of Venus

This sits right at the base of the thumb and is particularly noticeable. It indicates someone's level of vitality, sensuality and appreciation of beauty. If the mount is high, elastic and well developed, the person is outgoing and has a strong sex drive and plenty of physical energy. They will probably have artistic abilities and may even make their career in the arts. If the mount is extremely large, then these tendencies will be proportionately exaggerated.

An under-developed or flabby mount indicates someone who lacks vitality, may suffer from poor health, has a low sex drive and finds it difficult to express their emotions. (Describing this in tactful terms may take some doing!)

This mount also rules musical ability, shown by pronounced, angular joints at the base of the second phalange of the thumb and where the thumb joins the wrist. The upper joint relates to timing and the lower one to rhythm.

THE LINES OF THE HAND

A high proportion of people, even if they know nothing else about palmistry, can identify the major lines on their hands. Once you begin to

learn palmistry, you can spend many happy hours studying these lines. Some are clear and well defined, with few minor lines. Others are vague and sketchy, and may wander all over the place so that it's difficult to see where one line stops and another starts. Sometimes a line may be completely absent or so close to another that it's hard to tell them apart.

The basic lines found on the palm

The general rule for interpreting lines is the same as for the fingers and mounts – the stronger the line, the stronger the characteristics associated with it. If most of the lines on the hand are clear and well defined but one is weak, then the energies symbolized by this line don't flow properly. People whose lines are deep and strongly marked usually achieve a lot in life. Any interruptions to the line, such as breaks, chains or minor lines running across it, indicate problems and difficulties associated with the area of life denoted by the line. In other words, the energy of that line is being diffused or interrupted.

There are four major lines on the hand – the life line, the heart line, the head line and the fate line. Each shows how the person deals with a particular, important area of life.

THE LIFE LINE

This line usually starts between the thumb and Jupiter (index) finger on the edge of the palm and curves around the mount of Venus. It's extremely important as it shows the pattern of a person's life, and their strength, health and vitality. Landmarks in life – illnesses, accidents and changes in circumstance – appear on the life line.

Probably one of the first questions you'll be asked is, 'Will I live to a ripe old age?' Some people are concerned because they have short life lines and think this means a correspondingly short life, but it may not. If the line is clearly marked and runs strongly, the person will probably live a fairly long time. If, on the other hand, the line is short and weak, perhaps with feathering or chains, then the person will lack physical energy and may die relatively early. However, it is impossible to make any hard and fast rules about this because there may be mitigating factors elsewhere on the hand. Always err on the side of optimism when someone asks you how long they are going to live. Never tell them that they have a weak life line, or that they are likely to drop dead at any minute. Instead, suggest that they need to look after themselves.

Quality and Shape

Look first at the overall condition of the line. If it runs strongly and is a nice pink colour (a livid red indicates health problems), with few interruptions or chains, the person will enjoy good health and a long life. They have plenty of physical stamina and energy. A weak, pale line, or one that is crossed by lots of horizontal lines, that is chained or feathery or that has breaks in it, indicates poor health and lack of vitality. If most of the line is clear and only part of it is chained, broken or crossed by lines, the person will suffer from ill health during that period of their life. If the whole line is very faint and the hand is flabby, the person suffers from extremely poor health and is also highly strung and nervy.

Now look at the shape of the line. A generously curved line that sweeps around the mount of Venus and ends near the wrist indicates someone who is energetic and has a zest for life. They are warm-hearted, good at communicating with others, and able to survive whatever life throws at them. If the line only has a slight curve, the person finds it difficult to relate to others emotionally. They are inhibited, shy and introverted. If the line is straight and cuts through the mount of Venus, then the person is selfish, mean-spirited and cold-hearted.

A line that swings around the mount of Venus and then moves towards the mount of Luna shows a restless disposition. If, in addition, the hand is strong and the flesh is firm, the person will probably satisfy their itchy feet through travel. However, if the hand is weak and the flesh flabby, if there are many fine criss-cross lines on the plain of Mars and if the head line dips towards the mount of Luna, the person will fritter away their energies and never be organized enough to go travelling – it will be all talk and no action.

Beginning and Ending

Look to see where the line starts. If it begins on the mount of Jupiter, the person has been strongly ambitious from an early age. If the line starts low

on the hand, near the thumb, it indicates a limited imagination and a rather earthy temperament. When the head line and life line are joined together at the start, they show an inability to make decisions. This may be because the person is unduly influenced by family demands, or tied to their parents' apron strings, and therefore lacks confidence. If there's a moderate gap between the two lines, the person has a healthy sense of independence and confidence. A vast gap in between the two denotes a person who is head-strong and independent to the point of foolhardiness. This person may also be a keen gambler.

How does the life line end? If it becomes thinner and weaker, the person's energies will noticeably weaken as they near the end of their life. If it simply stops, ending as strongly as it began, the person will be in good health and fitness until the end of their life. If it ends curled around the bottom of the mount of Venus, it shows someone with a deep love of their home – it's their refuge, and they will always return to it as soon as they decently can. If the line ends in a fork, look to see where this points. If one fork points towards the mount of Luna, the person enjoys travelling but will always be pleased to come home again. If this fork is stronger or more dominant than the rest of the life line, the person will do a lot of travelling – whether physical or spiritual – or the circumstances of their life may alter dramatically.

An example of a broken life line

Breaks in the Line

Next, look for significant breaks in the line. These indicate accidents, changes of circumstance or extreme ill health. Be very careful when talking to someone with this mark in their hand because you don't want to frighten them or be unduly alarmist. Check whether the broken life line appears on the other hand as well – if so, the incident will profoundly affect the person. If the break only appears in one hand, the incident it foretells will not be so dramatic. If the life line does have a distinct break, look for small connecting lines between the two halves. Alternatively, the break may be enclosed by a square, or a sister line may run alongside it. All these markings indicate that the person will survive whatever it is that befalls them – the markings symbolize a bridge between the old life and the new. If there aren't any connecting lines at all, not even the finest, hair-like threads, then the event that the break foretells will have a powerful transforming effect on the person. It may also happen very suddenly, marking a complete change from the old life.

The shape of the break will also tell you a lot about the nature of the event. If the life line is thin and hugs the mount of Venus until it breaks, then becomes stronger and curves out towards the plain of Mars, the person will be much happier and feel more fulfilled after the change takes place – their life will expand. If, however, the

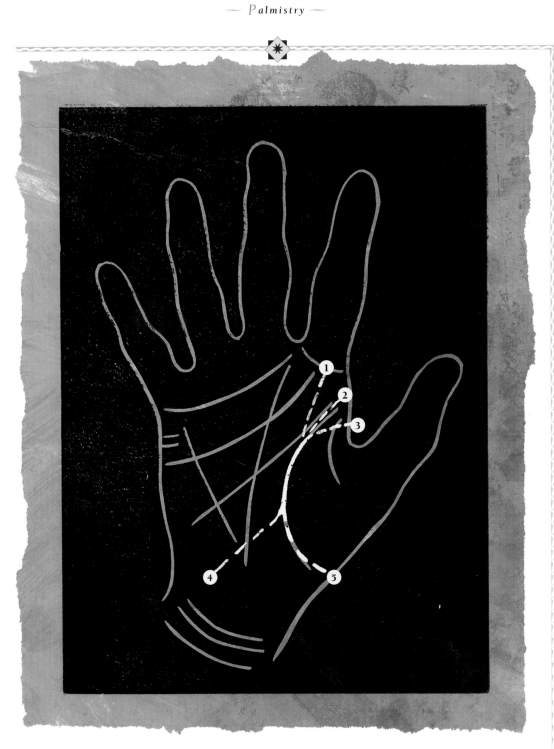

LIFE LINE

1 Begins on mount of Jupiter

2 Begins joined to head line

3 Begins joined to thumb

4 Forks to mount of Luna

5 Curls around mount of Venus

line is strong until it breaks, then continues as a pale line which runs straight or curves in towards the mount of Venus, there will be a change for the worse. Look at the head line and the thumb – if they are both strong, the person will be able to cope much better than someone with a small thumb and a weak head line.

Related Lines

One of the most fortunate markings on the life line is a sister line that runs beside it for part or all of its length (in which case it's called a double life line). This line acts as protection against any defects that appear in the life line, such as illnesses or changes of circumstance, and also boosts the person's vitality and energy. Traditionally, a sister line was believed to show the presence of a guardian angel in the person's life. (People rarely react negatively to this suggestion – they are generally delighted.)

It's most unusual to see a life line that's entirely free of marks. If you do, that person has either been astonishingly fortunate or, more likely, is so thick-skinned and insensitive that all of life's trials have simply bounced off them. Lines which rise from the life line indicate successes in life; lines which drop down indicate disappointments. Lines which cross it indicate obstacles. These could be either illnesses (especially if the line is weak at that particular point) or various other hurdles that must be surmounted.

THE HEART LINE

This line begins under the mount of Mercury and ends somewhere between the mounts of Jupiter and Saturn. As its name suggests, it denotes the emotional and physical state of a person's heart. The heart line is usually one of the easiest lines to read. And, since most people want to know about their love lives, it's also a popular one.

Quality and Shape

First of all, look at the quality of the line. If it's strong and clearly marked, with few interruptions or markings, it shows that the heart is in good physical condition. Unfortunately, it also indicates someone who's wrapped up in themselves and rather selfish; nevertheless, their emotions are constant. The fewer the lines that radiate out from the heart line, the less a person's affections go out to other people. If the line is light and insubstantial, the same applies to the person's emotions, and the health of their heart may not be all that good, either.

A chained heart line indicates someone whose emotional energies go round in circles but never result in anything. They may have a string of broken relationships because they fritter away their emotions and may be reluctant to commit themselves to one person.

Before you make any judgements about the quality of the line, look carefully at its shape, as this may have a mitigating effect. The normal heart line is curved, which shows sensitivity towards other people. Therefore, what appears to be a selfish heart line will in fact be less so if it's shaped like a crescent. The straighter the line is, the more insensitive the person is, and the more directly they will express all of their emotional needs, however self-centred.

Length

Now look at the length of the line. If it runs for a short distance and then stops abruptly, it shows someone who has felt only a limited range of emotions. Traditionally, it's believed that the person will experience difficulties at the time of life when the line ends. Either they will suffer from physical heart trouble or their feelings will be so badly hurt that they'll cut themselves off emotionally from other people.

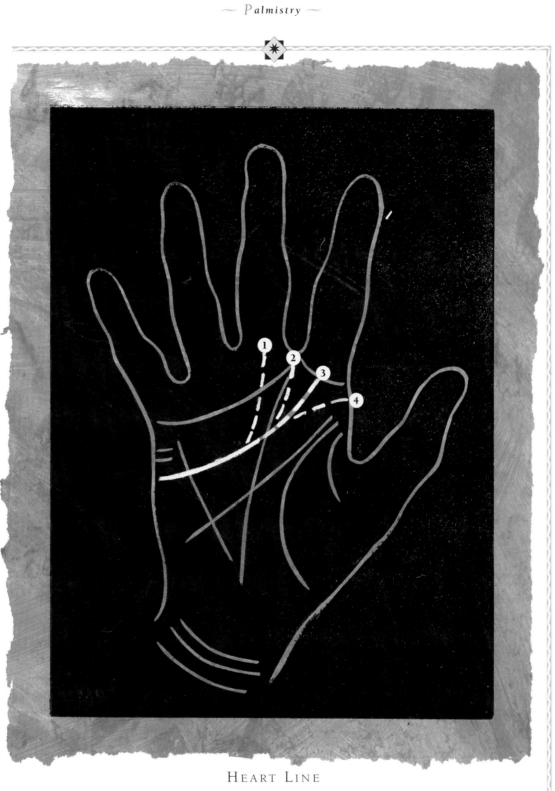

HEART LINE

1 Ends on mount of Saturn

2 Ends between Jupiter and Saturn fingers

3 Ends on mount of Jupiter

4 Ends on side of palm

If the line is abnormally long, running from one side of the palm to the other as if it's been wrapped around it, it shows someone who's ruled by their emotions, feels things passionately, and is prone to jealousy.

Beginnings and Endings

The heart line always starts somewhere under the mount of Mercury, on the outer edge of the palm. However, it can end in any one of four places on the hand – at the side of the palm under the mount of Jupiter, on the mount of Jupiter, between the index and second fingers, or on the mount of Saturn.

When the line ends at the side of the palm, it indicates someone who is jealous and possessive. Their heart line is extremely long, so they will experience a wide range of emotions in their life.

A line ending on the mount of Jupiter indicates someone who is an emotional idealist. They probably go through life suffering terrible disappointments when they discover that the people they idolized (and, in the process, idealized) have feet of clay after all. Supremely romantic, they would happily starve in a garret if that was the only way to be with their one true love. They are highly emotional and sensitive and are usually faithful and loyal.

If the line ends between the index and second fingers, it shows someone who's able to combine the emotional ardour indicated by the mount of Jupiter with the passion denoted by the mount of Saturn. Their emotions run calm and deep, and they take a sensible and practical approach to love. They are usually highly popular.

When the heart line ends on the mount of Saturn, the person is extremely passionate and sensual. Their emotions and sexual appetites usually get the better of them, and may cause problems at times. If the mount of Venus is large and well-coloured, the person's heart (and/or loins) rules their head.

Sometimes the heart line ends in a fork, in which case the person's emotions are a combination of the qualities denoted by the positions at which the fork ends. For instance, if one end of the fork rests between the index and second fingers, and the other sits on the mount of Jupiter, the person is good-natured and able to combine the practicality of the former position with the romantic tendencies of the latter. Look to see which branch of the fork is strongest, especially if there are three branches (which denote a very happy love life) – this will tell you which tendency predominates.

Occasionally the heart, head and life lines are joined together on the mount of Mars near the thumb. This isn't a good sign – it indicates emotional ruthlessness, someone who'll stop at nothing to get what they want from people because their thoughts, emotions and actions all spring from the same source.

Position

Does the heart line sit high on the hand or further down, almost touching the head line? If it's found high on the hand it indicates a sunny, happy nature. This person finds it easy to get on well with others and usually makes the best of any misfortunes that come their way.

If the heart line is low on the hand, it shows unhappy experiences in love. The person has a strong need to express their emotions physically.

If the heart line dips down so much that it crosses the head line and meets the life line, the person has so powerful a desire for physical contact that it could possibly lead to problems such as an abnormally high sex drive, some sort of sexual deviancy or, on rare occasions, even psychopathic tendencies.

Breaks in the Line

Are there any breaks in the heart line? If so, the same rule applies here as for the life line – look for links between the two halves. Breaks indicate the end of one phase in a person's emotional life and the start of another – this could be perhaps the end of a relationship, a divorce, or coming out if they are gay.

Unless you are practised in the art of medical hand analysis, do not ever attempt to diagnose a person's state of health from their heart line – or from any other line on the hand, come to that. The quality of the lines will tell you whether that person's physical energy flows well or poorly, but don't venture any deeper than that: you may frighten them or give them a false sense of security. Old palmistry books often give alarming explanations for various markings on the hand, such as brain fever, imminent death, paralysis, stabbing by a dark-haired woman wearing a pink cardigan, and so on. Ignore them all.

The Simian Line

Very occasionally, you'll be presented with a hand that has a single line running across the palm instead of separate heart and head lines. This is known as the simian line, and it indicates someone whose emotions and powers of reason are completely intertwined. This is a person who throws themselves completely wholeheartedly into experiences, sometimes with rather unfortunate results, because they cannot actually take an objective view of their actions: everything is approached with intensity.

The simian line – a combined head and heart line

THE HEAD LINE

This is the line that usually sits between the heart line and the life line. Rising on or near the life line and running across the plain of Mars before ending at a point somewhere under the Mercury finger, it indicates the quality of their intellect and reasoning ability.

Length and Quality

A short head line indicates someone whose reactions are much quicker than normal and who may at times make hasty judgements. If the line is very short (perhaps ending in the middle of the palm) or is weak or faint, this is said to denote a person who has poor mental abilities or finds it difficult to marshal their thoughts into any sort of order. They may also lack common sense or be easily swayed by other people.

The reverse is true if the line is well marked, doesn't fluctuate in strength and is long. Having

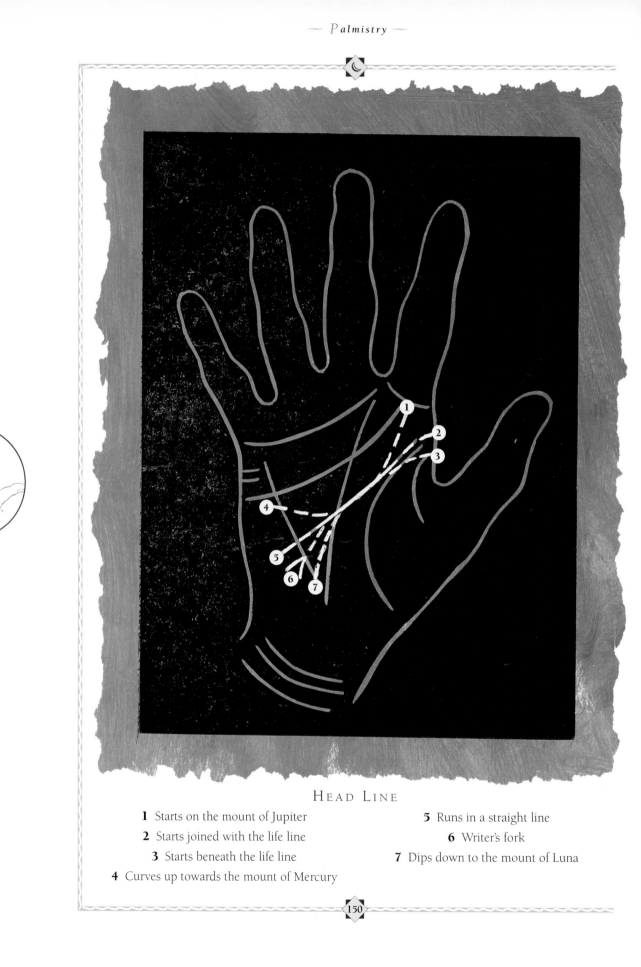

HEAD LINE

1 Starts on the mount of Jupiter

2 Starts joined with the life line

3 Starts beneath the life line

4 Curves up towards the mount of Mercury

5 Runs in a straight line

6 Writer's fork

7 Dips down to the mount of Luna

said that, someone with a very long head line can often become lost in thought – they take in so many impressions of the world around them that they need time to process them all. This means they are able to see both sides to every argument.

Now it's time to look at the line itself. Does it run in a firm, direct line, with no chains or islands along the way? This denotes someone who has fixed ideas and a well-balanced mind and who has a practical, commonsense approach to life.

A straight line that looks as if it's been drawn with a ruler right across the palm denotes someone who is very matter-of-fact and always takes an objective viewpoint. They have little imagination so they see life in extremely black and white terms.

If it's chained or feathered or wavers up and down for all or part of its length, the person finds it hard to concentrate and to think clearly for the period of time indicated by the markings. Islands on the line indicate periods of mental strain.

Look at where the head line rises on the hand. It begins from one of three places – on the mount of Jupiter, fused with the start of the life line, or beneath the life line.

If it rises on the mount of Jupiter, it indicates someone who is ambitious, self-confident and reliable. All things being equal, this person will enjoy a successful life.

If the head and life lines are joined together, the person lacks confidence and finds decision-making difficult because they are heavily influenced by family ties. The longer the distance for which the two lines are fused together, the more pronounced this tendency is, because the longer the influence of the family will be. If the two lines quickly move apart, the person will have established their independence at a young age.

Independence is a state of mind that's very foreign to someone whose head line rises beneath their life line. This person is extremely timid, insecure, withdrawn and nervous. They need constant reassurance that they're doing or saying the right thing, and they frequently change their minds. A sense of frustration with their lot may make them irritable.

Endings

Where does the line end? If it curves towards the mount of Luna, it shows a powerful, creative imagination but also a tendency to be gloomy at times. If the line dips steeply into this mount, the person can sometimes lose touch with reality, which may lead to depression.

Sometimes the head line ends by curving upwards towards one of the fingers, showing that the person is influenced by the area of life represented by that finger. If the line curves towards the Mercury finger, for example, the person is influenced by communications with others; if it curves towards the Apollo finger, they are influenced by their creative abilities.

If the line ends in a fork, traditionally this is said to be the writer's fork, and indicates a born writer. If the fork is extremely pronounced, with one end dipping towards the mount of Luna and the other running across the hand, it shows the ability to combine practicality with imagination. As always, look to see which branch is stronger and, therefore, which mental approach is dominant. On a good hand, this fork is an excellent sign; on a bad hand, it may indicate someone who is a born liar.

Breaks

Finally, look for breaks along the line and, if there are any, check for sister lines to connect the two halves of the break. If there is also a break in the life or heart line at the same place as in the head line, you can safely assume that the person will experience a dramatic change in circumstance at the time of the break that will affect all areas of their life. If the break is confined to the head line only, they will change their minds about something in a most profound way.

THE FATE LINE

This is also called the line of Saturn, because it normally runs up the palm from the base of the hand towards the finger of Saturn. It relates to worldly affairs, the career, success or failure and the people who influence our lives for good or ill.

Presence or Absence

Some people don't have a line of fate, while for others it may feature strongly in one hand and very faintly in the other. The partial or complete lack of a fate line doesn't imply a lack of destiny – it means that the person dislikes routine and doesn't plan much in their life, preferring to let things take their course. The presence of a strong fate line indicates someone who is reliable, is sympathetic to the idea of a regular routine, and has a certain amount of inner drive and ambition. They are better able to steer their life in roughly the direction they want it to take, whether they do this consciously or not.

If there's a fate line on the hand that the person writes with, but not on the other one, they direct a lot of conscious effort into achieving their desires. If it's only on the non-writing hand, they may have splendid dreams of success which they never bother to put into action.

When you look at this line on someone's palm, always bear in mind that it symbolizes the direction of their life as a whole, and not just their career. Also remember that success comes in many forms and is extremely subjective – what may seem a dreary, unexciting life to you may be highly fulfilling and rewarding to someone else.

Beginnings and Endings

Unlike the other major lines on the hand, the fate line can start and end in any number of ways. As a general rule, the higher on the hand that the fate line starts, the later the person will start to feel ambitious, find their direction in life or become able to achieve their objectives. Equally, a line starting at the wrist denotes someone who knew what they wanted to achieve at an early age. This is especially true if the line is firmly etched into the hand at this point.

If the fate line starts within the life line, on the mount of Venus, the person will do what their family expects of them until the line breaks free and moves out into the plain of Mars. This is a classic indication of the person who felt dutybound to go into the family firm or follow a career that their parents chose for them.

If the line starts on the mount of Luna, the person has been independent and has known what they want to do in life from an early age – and it's probably something that uses their creative imagination. What's more, it will often put them in the public eye.

Where does the line end? If it rises from the wrist and marches straight up the hand towards the mount of Saturn, the person will enjoy success and great good fortune. If it climbs so high that it touches the finger of Saturn, the person will carry on working until way past normal retirement age.

If it rises from the wrist and climbs to a different mount, the person will experience success in whichever area is denoted by that mount.

If the fate line changes direction, having crossed the heart line, and runs up to the mount of Jupiter, the person is dedicated to their work and will enjoy enormous success and power – this is someone who stands out from the crowd. In fact, any branches from the fate line towards

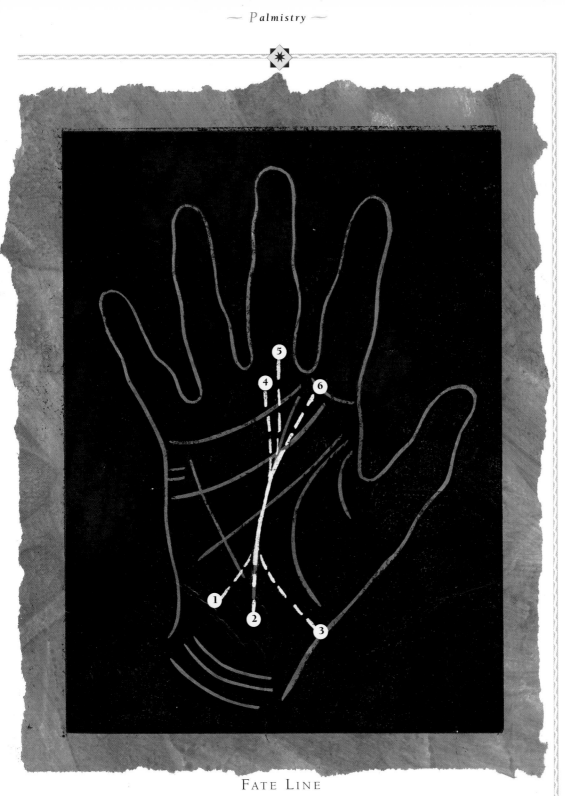

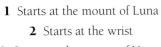

FATE LINE

1 Starts at the mount of Luna   4 Ends on the mount of Saturn

2 Starts at the wrist   5 Ends on the Saturn finger

3 Starts on the mount of Venus   6 Ends on the mount of Jupiter

the mount of Jupiter are an excellent sign, and show success at whichever stage of life in which they occur.

If the line finishes at the heart line, it shows that an emotional disappointment will bring an end to the person's ambitions. If it finishes at the head line, the ambitions will end through a lack of sound judgement or reasoning.

Quality

The condition of the line will, of course, tell you a great deal about the nature of the person's career and direction in life. Sometimes you'll see a line that has several marked breaks in it, denoting changes in direction. If the breaks run parallel to one another, the person will combine the old career or way of life with the new one for the duration of the overlap. They may not even be aware of the change in direction until it's completed. Breaks without overlaps indicate sudden changes in life. If the line is very faint and feathery, the person will fritter their energies away on various ventures that never come to anything. Islands in the line denote times when the person loses direction or purpose. Bars that cross the line indicate obstacles or interruptions, especially if they link up with the life line.

THE MINOR LINES

There are many minor lines on the hand, but certain ones are more important. Not all of these lines appear on each hand – some hands (especially Earth ones) may have none while others will have some or all of them.

The Line of Mercury

Sometimes called the hepatic or health line, this line starts at the base of the hand and runs out towards the mount of Mercury. Curiously enough, tradition dictates that you're better off without this line – its absence means that you've no need to worry about your health. When the line is present, it indicates someone who must ensure they get plenty of rest and who can become ill through stress. It is linked with the liver and the blood (hence its old name, the hepatic line), so a weak line may indicate problems in these areas. The stronger the line, the healthier the person.

The Line of Mars

This is a good line to have, because it denotes strong vitality and energy, and also excellent powers of recuperation after illness. However, there's nothing sinister to be deduced from its absence. It begins somewhere between the life line and the thumb and runs down the mount of Venus, parallel to the life line. It can be long or short. Traditionally, this line is said to protect against jealousy, which is just as well because it's believed to bestow great talents in the career which can in turn provoke jealousy in people who are less gifted.

A gypsy reading a woman's palm

The Ring of Solomon

Here's another excellent line. It curves around the base of the Jupiter finger (don't confuse it with the line between the base of the finger and the palm), or sits on the mount. The deeper and better-formed the line, the better the person is at understanding others and tuning into them. It is therefore an excellent line for teachers, writers, counsellors, therapists, doctors and lawyers. This ability to tune into others can also be expressed in psychic ability and an interest in the occult.

The Bracelets of Neptune

Found at the base of the wrist, these lines traditionally denote good luck, especially when there are four of them – the normal ration is two. Whatever their number, they indicate good health if they are well defined. Chained bracelets mean a lack of stamina. When the top bracelet arches up into the base of the wrist, it denotes problems with the internal organs.

The Girdle of Venus

Not to be confused with a double heart line, the girdle of Venus is a curved line that sits high on the palm, above the heart line. It normally runs from the Jupiter or Saturn finger to the Apollo or Mercury finger, and indicates a passionate nature. This may be expressed as sexual passion or possibly devotion to a particular interest or vocation. It indicates heightened emotions, especially if the line is strong and deep, and denotes sensitivity.

The Lines of Marriage

Lots of people get excited about these lines, because they are said to be the traditional indicators of marriage. Today, they generally represent important relationships which have had a profound impact on the person – these may not necessarily be marriages.

Look for one or more short horizontal lines on the outside of the palm, between the base of the Mercury finger and the heart line. If you can't see them very clearly, curl up the fingers slightly and the lines will become more obvious. The stronger the line, the more important the relationship. However, if you only see one line, don't assume that the person has only experienced one relationship – they may have had many, but only one will have meant a great deal to them. If the lines are close together, the relationships have more or less followed on from each other; big gaps indicate several years between the relationships. Vertical lines rising from the marriage lines are said to indicate children, although it would be more accurate to say that they signify the desire to have children, which may or may not be fulfilled.

RANDOM LINES

Unless you are looking at a classic Earth hand, with very few lines on it, you'll notice that the palm is dotted with several subsidiary markings. Some of these are single lines, while others form shapes such as triangles, crosses or stars. It's beyond the scope of this book to describe what each of these markings means in every position in the hand, but a few basic guidelines are given here. If necessary, use your initiative and intuition, combining your knowledge of the general significance of the marking with that of the part of the hand that's affected. These random patterns can be interesting but they are not vital when you are first learning how to read palms because whatever it is that they signify will also appear elsewhere in the hand.

The Square

This is a protective marking, especially if it's formed around a line (whether broken or not). A square helps to minimize any potential harm or danger to a person. If the square appears on a mount, it somewhat reduces the negative qualities of that mount. For instance, a square on the mount of Saturn gives protection against pessimism and morbidity. A square on the mount of Jupiter has special significance because it denotes a born teacher.

The Star

Although you might imagine that stars denote good fortune, they are generally believed to have unfavourable meanings, signifying shocks or upsets connected with the area of life ruled by their position on the palm. So, a star on the mount of Jupiter means a shock or a severe disappointment connected with ambition, while on the mount of Venus it means unhappiness through love. As usual, there is an exception to the rule – a star on the mount of Apollo signifies success in the arts.

The Cross

As its name suggests, a cross is not a good sign, yet, curiously, it's one of the most common of all random markings. It's sometimes formed from a stray line crossing one of the main lines of the hand, but it may also be independent of any other lines. A cross signifies an obstacle or defect that has to be surmounted. Therefore, a cross on the mount of Luna signifies problems connected with the imagination – perhaps the person often makes mountains out of molehills. The more strongly marked the cross, the greater its significance.

The Triangle

This has to be well marked to be worthy of any consideration, otherwise it should be completely ignored. It is an extremely favourable sign, indicating mental brilliance. A triangle on the mount of Mercury, therefore, signifies that the person is brilliant at communicating their ideas. If someone has a triangle on the mount of Venus, they are lucky in love.

The Grille

Sadly, we've now returned to the subject of unfavourable markings. The grille is formed by a network of horizontal and vertical lines which cross each other at right angles. The finer the lines that make up the grille, the less significant it, and its effects, will be. It symbolizes obstacles in life which have to be surmounted, and which relate to the area of life that is ruled by that part of the hand. Therefore, a grille on the mount of Saturn indicates a tendency towards melancholy and pessimism, which can blight the person's life.

PREDICTING EVENTS

When you read palms, some people will be content with an in-depth character analysis while others will ask you what their future holds. This is an easy question to answer when you can see that their life will be a happy and satisfying one, but what should you do if you spot something awful in someone's hand? For example, you might see a severely broken life line which suggests a terrible accident or an irreversible change in their circumstances. The answer is simple – you issue a general warning but you don't frighten the person. You certainly don't drop their hand with a shriek or advise them to get all their affairs in order, pronto. Give them a few tactful hints along the right lines, perhaps suggesting that their financial affairs need sorting out or that they should take better care of their health. Even if you're asked whether you can see anything bad, you should still be diplomatic. Never make negative, upsetting predictions. Bear in mind that future events that are shown on the hand do not

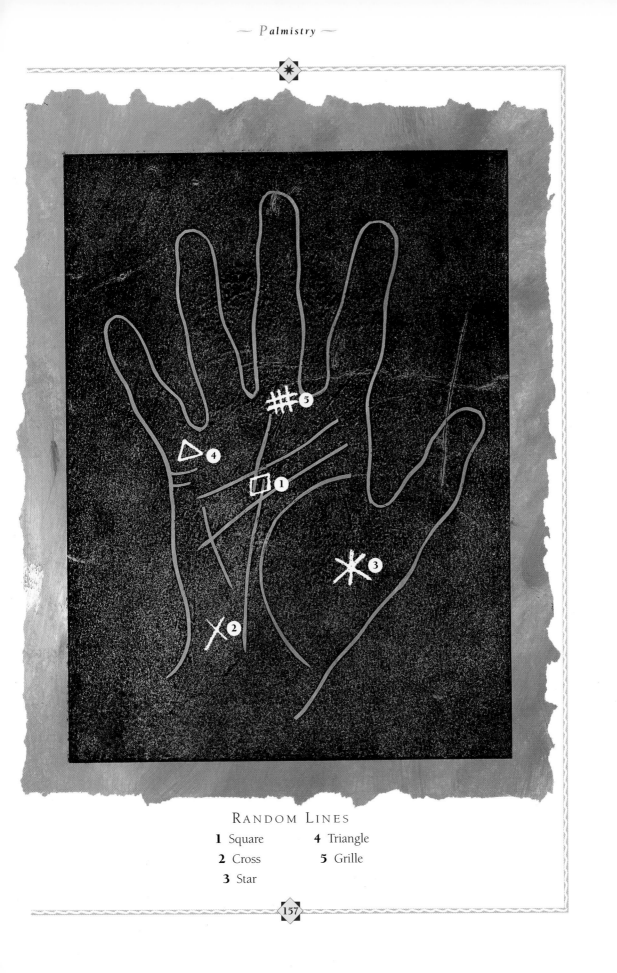

RANDOM LINES

1 Square **4** Triangle

2 Cross **5** Grille

3 Star

always take place – the person may take avoiding action, in which case the lines will alter over time to reflect this.

Also refrain from making moral judgements about what you see. State the facts and leave it at that. For instance, if the person is married but they are obviously going to have an affair, you can say that they will have a strong emotional relationship with someone but you shouldn't make them feel guilty about it.

Palmists are often asked if the lines on the hand change over the years. Yes, they do. Lines arrive or vanish, according to the path your life is taking. If you take prints or photocopies of your own hands every year or so, you'll see for yourself that some lines become more prominent and others get fainter or vanish altogether.

A popular French palmistry manual from the early twentieth century

Finally, always remember that the person who has asked you to give a reading is investing a lot of faith in you. Even people who laugh about having their palms read and appear to take it as a joke soon change their minds once you start to give them an accurate reading. They will probably give your words immense significance. While gratifying, this means you should choose those words carefully when issuing warnings or describing negative character traits.

TIMING EVENTS

Giving the exact timing of events is extremely difficult because no two hands are the same. If you know that certain events shown in the hand have already taken place, you can ask the person how old they were when these happened and use them as a guideline when timing future events.

The diagram shown here gives you a rough idea of how to date events along each line, based on the premise that the average lifespan is 75 years. Obviously, if you are reading the palm of a 90-year-old, you'll have to revise this dating system accordingly. There are some very complicated systems for timing events, some of which include putting rulers across the hand and measuring lines exactly, but these tend to confuse an issue which is already complex enough. You'll find that once you've read a few palms and you become more confident, your intuition will start to guide you.

Avoid timing events from the wrong end of a line – remember that the life and head lines rise from the thumb, while the heart line rises from the percussion side of the hand. The fate and health lines rise from the wrist. When timing marriage lines, do so from the heart line up towards the Mercury finger. If a major or minor line is very short, divide that part of the palm, not the line itself, into four.

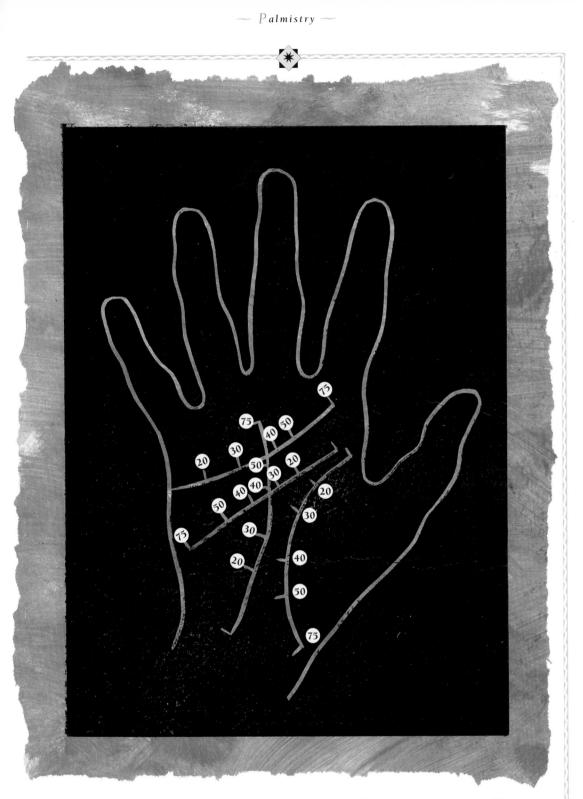

The lines of the hand can be divided into segments corresponding to periods of a person's life,
allowing the timing of the events shown in the hand to be predicted

Numerology

What's in a name? Everything, as it turns out. The name by which you

are known can, when reduced to numbers, influence your destiny,

and there are many tales of people whose luck changed for the

better when they altered the spelling of their names. Your date

of birth, which can't be altered legally, can also reveal a great

deal about your character. Once you have assessed your own

numbers, you can use numerology to discover your compatibility

with friends and family, and to choose a suitable name for your

children, your pets or even your house.

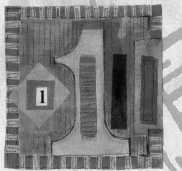

For AS LONG AS WE have been able to count, numbers have been a source of fascination. The Babylonians, Phoenicians and Hebrews all believed in the power and significance of numbers. It was the Greek mathematician and astrologer Pythagoras (c.580–c.500 BC), who first put forward the theory that everything in life, from music to one's name, could be symbolized and ruled by a number. Despite the fact that many cultures and people later developed his ideas, Pythagoras is considered to be the father of numerology, and his Pythagorean school was the cradle from which our present-day numerology stems.

One of his theories, which is still followed in numerology, is that odd numbers have positive or masculine qualities while even numbers are negative or feminine. Therefore, odd numbers are considered to be outgoing, active and full of energy; even numbers are sensitive, yielding and passive.

In numerology, only 11 numbers are used – from 1 to 9, plus 11 and 22. Any other number is reduced to one of these numbers by adding the digits together. For instance, 37 is reduced by adding 3 and 7 together to make 10, and then 1 and 0 are added together to give 1. (The numbers 11 and 22 are known as master numbers because, even though they have two digits, they are not reduced any further.) Numerology is a way of looking at numbers that enables you to analyse not only the meaning of your name and birthdate, but also other numbers in your life.

Numerological square used as an amulet

LIVING BY NUMBERS

Do certain numbers crop up in your life with astonishing regularity? For instance, if you were born on the 4th, you might find that this number seems to carry a lot of significance in your life. The number of your house might add up to four, you might have four children or your partner might also have been born on the 4th. Numerology will give you some clues as to why this should happen, by telling you the significance of the number four (it symbolizes stability and reliability) and showing you how to discover the numerical significance of any name that figures in your life, as well as any birthdate.

This chapter will show you how to discover four different numbers in your life:

❖ Your destiny number, from your date of birth

❖ Your personality number, from the name by which you're usually known

❖ Your heart number, from the vowels that are in that name

❖ Your expression number, from the consonants that are in that name

DESTINY NUMBER
You calculate the destiny number from your date of birth. It is a very significant number because you can't change it legally (even if you tell everyone that you're younger or older than you really are), and it reveals the sort of lessons you will

have to learn during the course of your life. If you believe in karma, the Eastern belief that your current actions determine your future, you could consider this to be your karmic number.

It's extremely easy to calculate your destiny number. Simply add up all the numbers in your birthdate until you reach any number between 1 and 9, or 11 or 22.

John Lennon

Let's say you want to find the destiny number of John Lennon, who was born on 9 October 1940. Write down the date in numerical form and add all the numbers together (you can just ignore the noughts), then add up the numbers in this result in order to reach the final number:

$$9 + 1 + 1 + 9 + 4 = 24$$
$$2 + 4 = 6$$

So, his destiny number is Six.

Incidentally, if you have added or subtracted a few years from your real birthdate, you should calculate both dates. The destiny number of your real birthdate will tell you about your true self, while that of your assumed birthdate will reveal a great deal about the way you would like to be seen by others.

PERSONALITY NUMBER

This number, taken from the name by which you are usually known, shows your natural abilities and talents, your strengths and weaknesses.

If you dislike your real first name and are always known by a nickname, then you should use this to calculate your personality number.

Equally, if your real name is Susan but you are always known as Sue, that is the name you should use. Ignore any middle names, unless they form part of the name by which you are always known.

Now imagine that you want to calculate John Lennon's personality number. His original full name was, in fact, John Winston Lennon, but he later changed this to John Ono Lennon. So which name should you use? Actually, because he was known simply as John Lennon, that is the name you should use to calculate his personality number. If he had preferred to call himself Ono Lennon, or if he had only ever been known by his surname, those would be the names that you would use.

Now you need to convert the letters of the name into numbers, using the following system, known as the Pythagorean system.

1	2	3	4	5	6	7	8	9
A	B	C	D	E	F	G	H	I
J	K	L	M	N	O	P	Q	R
S	T	U	V	W	X	Y	Z	

Numerologists disagree about whether Y counts as a vowel or a consonant. Some say it's always a consonant while others believe that its pronunciation is the determining factor. So, when they calculate the name Yolande, Y acts as a consonant, but when Y is pronounced in the same way as a vowel, as in Holly, that is how you should count it. You can experiment with names and see which system works best for you. However, there is an unbreakable rule for a name without any vowels, such as Lynch – always count the Y as a vowel, whether it's pronounced that way or not.

First, write down the name, then put the numerical value of each letter either above or below it. Write the numbers for the vowels above the name, and those for the consonants below it.

```
6              5        6
J  O  H  N     L  E  N  N  O  N
1     8  5     3     5  5     5
```

You are now ready to add up the numbers. Start with the vowels in the name:

$$6 + 5 + 6 = 17$$

This number is too high for the purposes of numerology, so it has to be reduced by adding the two digits together:

$$1 + 7 = 8$$

So, all the vowels in the name add up to Eight. This is the heart number, which will be described more fully later on in this chapter.

The next step is to calculate the numerical value of the consonants:

$$1 + 8 + 5 + 3 + 5 + 5 + 5 = 32$$

Again, this number is too high, so you have to reduce it:

$$3 + 2 = 5$$

So, all the consonants add up to Five. This is the expression number, which also will be described in more detail later in this chapter.

All that is left to do now is to add the numerical value of the vowels and consonants together to find the personality number:

$$8 + 5 = 13$$
$$1 + 3 = 4$$

So, John Lennon's personality number is Four.

HEART NUMBER

This is calculated from the vowels in a name. It gives an extra depth of meaning to the personality number by revealing the person's innermost desires, the way they would like to be in a perfect world and what they may fantasize about. The heart number is the private side of the personality, so when you calculate it for someone else you may not recognize this facet of their character.

In the example given for John Lennon, his heart number is Eight.

EXPRESSION NUMBER

This is calculated from the numerical value of the consonants in a person's name. It reveals the way they react to the world and the face they present to other people. This may be a reflection of their inner self or it might be a completely different facet of their personality.

In the example given for John Lennon, his expression number is Five.

PUTTING IT ALL TOGETHER

Once you have all this information you can start to gain more insight into your own personality, and also that of the people whose numbers you calculate. For instance, you may discover why you don't get on well with some people, or the reason you feel drawn to others. You'll also be able to know yourself better, which is, after all, the key to successful communication.

It is most harmonious for someone if their destiny and personality numbers are either both odd or both even. You may be able to change slightly the spelling of your name, or introduce an initial, to turn your name into an even or odd number that harmonizes with your destiny number. This enables the energies of the two numbers to work better together, with the result that your life will run more smoothly.

You can also use numerology to find the most auspicious name for a company you want to set up, a child, your house, or your young brother's rock group. Some numbers (especially Eight) are ideally suited for business; others (such as Nine) are very creative but may need some solid backbone in the form of willpower and determination (which is when you need to look carefully at the expression and heart numbers).

When you're familiar with the meanings of each number, you might like to read the interpretations of John Lennon's four numbers, because together they present some surprising insights into his character. They also demonstrate

something that you'll quickly realize when you study numerology in more depth – many people have contradictory or very different numbers, some of which may be difficult to reconcile with the person concerned unless you know a lot about their life. For instance, John Lennon's destiny number is Six – a home-loving number you might not associate with someone renowned for their creativity, restlessness and ascerbic wit (qualities that are vividly reflected in his expression number of Five). But this makes sense once you know that he spent his last years in New York simply being a house-husband, baking bread and looking after his son Sean. He was apparently extremely happy.

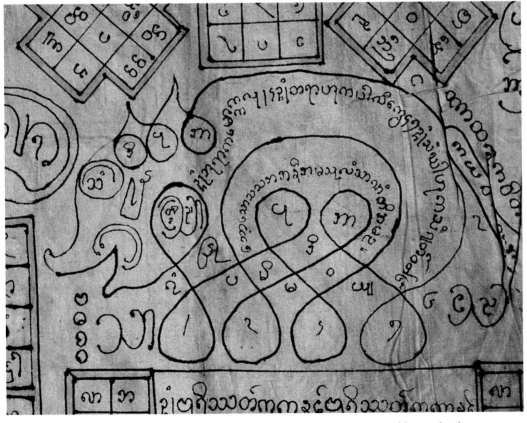

Top: numerological talisman. Above: amuletic shirt worn to protect soldiers in battle

ONE

A very powerful number, this represents unity and wholeness. It is the first masculine number. One is the number of beginnings and is therefore considered to be the number of God and the universe. It symbolizes the Sun, so is linked to Leo. Its colours are orange, yellow and gold.

DESTINY NUMBER

This is the number of the pioneer, the complete original. Anyone whose birthdate adds up to One is determined to go their own way; they're independent, inventive, opinionated and enthusiastic. They may even have ideas that are ahead of their time. You can't restrict these people because they will always find a way to express themselves and to realize their ambitions – their personality

number will tell you what direction these aims might take. Sometimes this perseverance can turn into obstinacy, bossiness and a single-mindedness that wins them few friends.

Ones are not good members of teams, unless they're calling the shots. They are natural leaders, which may explain why people approach

them with caution at first – Ones automatically take control of a situation. However, once you get to know them, you discover their kind, affectionate and genial side.

PERSONALITY NUMBER

These people are forceful, innovative and freedom-loving, very much like those whose destiny number is One. They may be slow starters in life but once they get going there's no stopping them, especially if they use their creativity. In fact, they react very badly to any sort of restriction, especially if One is also their destiny number. They need plenty of change in their lives because of the stimulation it brings them.

HEART NUMBER

No matter what this person's other numbers are, nor how they lead their life, they have an inner vision of themselves as an innovator and a leader. They're ambitious, energetic and highly confident – it can be a waste of time giving them advice because they are not likely to take it. It may be difficult to get close to them emotionally because they can take love for granted. They may also feel superior to other people, even if they would never dream of admitting it.

EXPRESSION NUMBER

The first thing you notice about this person is their confidence. They usually appear very sure of themselves (so much so, that sometimes this comes across as arrogance), even if their other numbers tell a different story. They are popular and find it easy to make friends. If you ever feel a crisis coming on, seek out someone with this number – their supportive, don't-worry-it'll-all-be-OK attitude will help you through.

TWO

This is the dual number, the number of Yin and Yang, masculinity and femininity, night and day, and all other opposites. Harmony, rhythm and diplomacy are associated with Two. It symbolizes the Moon, so is linked to the sign of Cancer and pearlescent colours.

DESTINY NUMBER

This is the first passive number. These people function best in a harmonious partnership but are likely to concede too much power in arguments – they believe in the maxim 'anything for a quiet life'. Eventually, this may make them resentful and depressed. They are highly supportive, preferring to take a back seat while others strive for the top. In relationships, they are considerate and loving but can be moody. Anything with a strong rhythm, such as music or poetry, is an excellent way to help them unwind.

PERSONALITY NUMBER

Here is someone who is tactful, diplomatic and able to soothe hurt feelings. This makes them invaluable in situations that need careful arbitration, because they're skilled negotiators. However, they tend to retreat into their shells at the first sign of difficulty – they probably consider this to be protective action although others may construe it as sulking. These people like to hold on to relationships, belongings, jobs or anything else that they value, sometimes long after they should have moved on to something new. This is because of their emotional sensitivity, which can make them overly protective of loved ones.

HEART NUMBER

Appearances are deceptive for people with this heart number because, no matter how self-assured and confident they may appear, underneath they are extremely sensitive and easily hurt. They tend to retreat from unpleasant situations but will do their utmost to try to prevent these from ever happening at all – emotional security is vitally important to them. This person is a wonderfully supportive and sympathetic partner and friend who will be there for you through thick and thin.

EXPRESSION NUMBER

Relationships are very important to these people, often to such an extent that they continually look for perfection rather than enjoy what they already have. Partners may quickly tire of this critical streak – Two needs to learn to relax and trust their loved ones, and also to allow things to go wrong sometimes, accepting that this is an inevitable part of life. They are an excellent member of a team, perfectly happy to work in the background while someone else basks in the spotlight.

THREE

The number Three is associated with spring, and consequently with beginnings, new ventures and with fertile phases of growth. These can be physical or mental. Three is symbolized by the triangle and can therefore represent the Holy Trinity. It is linked to the planet Jupiter, the sign Sagittarius, and the colours mauve and amethyst.

DESTINY NUMBER

This person enjoys happy and productive relationships. Despite being born flirts, for whom fidelity may not always be top of the list of priorities (even though they might expect it in return), they have deep-seated feelings for partners. They are happy-go-lucky, warm, cheerful, sociable and optimistic, with a gift for words. Threes enjoy family life although they do not appreciate feeling hemmed in by drudgery or too many responsibilities. Travel is important to them, as is a need for challenge – they would hate to think that life is passing them by.

PERSONALITY NUMBER

Threes are creative, skilled communicators and extremely good company. They're extrovert, charming, cheerful and optimistic – things are always going to get better. And Threes often do enjoy considerable success, especially if their career puts them in the public eye or capitalizes on their ability to communicate. Clothes are important, although they prefer to dress in their own style rather than to follow fashion slavishly. Threes need to lead a busy, varied life otherwise they will become jaded and bored. The same goes for relationships – anything that becomes too much of a routine, too predictable or restricting will make them unhappy, and could then send them off in search of pastures new.

HEART NUMBER

It is very enjoyable to be around this person. Cheerful and good fun, they are strongly confident that everything will turn out well in the end, and it usually does. This person is a warm and supportive friend and partner, full of encouragement and always happy to see others succeed. Threes have a terrific sense of humour that buoys up everyone around them, including themselves,

and makes them very popular. However, this joviality may hide a darker side of their personality which craves love and fears rejection.

EXPRESSION NUMBER

When you meet this person you are immediately struck by their confidence, bonhomie and generous spirit. They adore being in the limelight and will often be the pivot around which the conversation revolves. This Three is an instinctive performer but may not be such a good audience – for example, they may not be a very patient listener. Sometimes they can become boastful and arrogant, especially if they are feeling nervous.

FOUR

This number is symbolized by the four points of the compass and the four seasons. As a result, Four is associated with foundations, with a sense of structure and tradition, and therefore with the sign of Capricorn. Its planetary ruler is Saturn, and its colours are dark greys and blacks.

DESTINY NUMBER

This person has the discipline and willpower to achieve whatever they want out of life and to make the most of their potential. At first, their life may seem to be limited and restricted in some way, but once they are able to come to terms with this they can achieve a great deal. Any job that enables a Four to develop their wonderful organizational skills will not only benefit themselves but also the people around them. Whatever they do for a living, they need to bring out their practical nature. Fours should guard against becoming too rigid, narrow-minded, stern or zealous. They need to remember that there is room in life for enjoyment as well as for work.

PERSONALITY NUMBER

People born under this number love order and structure. They feel edgy when they aren't sure of what the future holds, and they like their lives to be stable, organized and built on a solid foundation. Fours are immensely practical and are always dependable in crises. However, they must avoid taking themselves – or life – too seriously, otherwise their reliability and common sense can turn into a rather peevish, pessimistic approach. This number is closely associated with nature, so it's important for Fours to spend time outdoors.

HEART NUMBER

Here is someone whose deep shyness means they prefer to stand in the shadows rather than be thrown into the spotlight. However, they won't be idle – instead, they will be making the most of their tremendous practical abilities and immense organizational talents to ensure that life runs as smoothly as possible. This is someone you can truly rely upon. Fours are happiest in secure environments, preferably with a good, steady job as well as a comfortable, solid home life. They are wary of change and can sometimes become stuck in too much of a rut.

EXPRESSION NUMBER

This person is the salt of the earth – reliable, practical, dependable and trustworthy. As a result, they may resemble a workhorse. For instance, this is the personal assistant who quietly gets on with their job but whose organizational skills ensure the smooth-running of the entire office – the place would fall apart without them. Their innate conservatism makes them mistrustful of people they consider to be lacking in moral fibre or outrageous in some way, and they can sometimes be narrow-minded, unimaginative and frightened of change.

FIVE

This number is connected with freedom and movement, energy, creativity and travel. It is symbolized by the pentacle, the five-pointed star. Five is linked with Mercury, and therefore with Gemini and Virgo. It rules all pale colours.

DESTINY NUMBER

These people are extremely lively and restless. They will happily try everything at least once, and enjoy a life that is full of variety and change. Travel appeals to them, especially if they get the chance to visit new destinations and places that are exciting and demand a spirit of adventure. They have a strong intellect and excellent powers of communication, both of which they should put to good use in their career – they are particularly good at dealing with the public. Fives are witty, chatty, charming and versatile, but run the risk of becoming restless and being jacks of all trades, masters of none.

PERSONALITY NUMBER

Adventure is the lifeblood of this person. They need to keep on the move and they can't bear the thought of life becoming stagnant or boring. Every so often they are compelled to make major changes in their lives, despite the effects this might have on the people around them. At times, they may even introduce change purely for its own sake. This can lead to recklessness and a dare-devil approach to life. Fives are always looking ahead, to the next job, the next holiday – sometimes even to the next love affair (they are not known for their fidelity). They love travel and may even emigrate.

HEART NUMBER

No matter how stable or sensible this person appears on the surface, it's a different story underneath. They may feel an underlying dissatisfaction and a nagging sense that life could be much more exciting if only they knew how to make it so. Not surprisingly, this restlessness may adversely affect their relationships. Fives may find it difficult to deal with authority figures, especially if such people are restrictive or dictatorial. Fives' liveliness, charm and versatility wins them many friends, but they must be on the same intellectual wavelength. Fives may underestimate their mental abilities when young, so it's only later in their lives that they study subjects in depth.

EXPRESSION NUMBER

This person is inquisitive, restless and good fun to have around. Fives are excellent company because they always seem to know a little about everything and are very interested in their friends' lives. Too interested, sometimes, as they have a tendency to gossip and get involved in things that aren't any of their business. Nevertheless, their broad knowledge, intellectual abilities and lively character win them plenty of respect and popularity. They are also full of surprises and dislike staying in one relationship, house, job or country for too long – now you see them, now you don't.

SIX

This is an extremely harmonious number, associated with love, service, responsibility and balance. It is symbolized by the six-pointed star and linked to the planet Venus, and therefore the two signs Taurus and Libra. Its colours are pale blues, turquoises and greens.

stamina and desire to do well. These people are loving and need a harmonious relationship, yet they can be intolerant of people who don't measure up to their high standards, not only emotionally but also physically and sartorially.

DESTINY NUMBER

This is the natural homemaker, someone who needs a stable domestic life and a loving family around them in order to feel contented and emotionally secure. They may spend so much time ensuring the comfort and happiness of their nearest and dearest that they neglect their own needs, which can occasionally make them feel resentful and taken for granted. They can also become very insular, only concentrating on their immediate social circle. At work, they are reliable members of a team and have an excellent eye for detail. They need to guard against possessiveness, selfishness and jealousy, which can mar an otherwise attractive and loving personality.

PERSONALITY NUMBER

This person is an instinctive helper of others, someone who needs to be of service. They may express this through their job (which may be a vocation), their family life or the way they fill their spare time. As a result, they are usually given plenty of responsibility, although they may take this to extremes at times by becoming too perfectionist and nit-picking. They find it easy to handle money and are especially successful when they're self-employed – they have the requisite

HEART NUMBER

Extremely kind-hearted, considerate and loving, these people make excellent partners, colleagues, parents and friends. They are very good at taking care of other people's needs, whether or not it's expected of them. They demand the same consideration in return and are rarely disappointed, which is just as well because otherwise they will feel insecure and lacking in confidence. Because their domestic family life is so important to them, they may choose to work from home as they will then be available whenever they're needed. They are strongly creative and artistic.

EXPRESSION NUMBER

Luxury-loving and sybaritic, these people enjoy the best that life has to offer. They are naturally drawn to the smartest restaurants, biggest shows and swankiest bars, whether or not they can afford them. One thing they are rarely short of is good company, thanks to their charismatic personalities. They have a very easygoing attitude to life, which can mean they will go out of their way to avoid trouble or unpleasantness – a trait that may be emphasized if they have the Sun in Taurus or Libra. As a result, Sixes can be rather selfish, which is a characteristic they need to watch.

SEVEN

The mystical number Seven is associated with philosophy, spiritual insights and inner contemplation. Seven is linked with Neptune, and therefore the sign of Pisces. Its colours are sea greens and aquamarines.

DESTINY NUMBER

These people have psychic abilities which they may use professionally or might experience as periodic hunches and uncanny intuitions. They are extremely sensitive, not only to the feelings of loved ones and the world around them but also to emotional undercurrents. For instance, their dreams may be particularly vivid and significant. They also have powerful imaginations that can lead them into escapism or flights of fantasy, sometimes with unfortunate results. Sevens are contemplative, introspective and may become quite remote and withdrawn at times; this can set them apart from others. They tend to worry, which can badly affect their health.

PERSONALITY NUMBER

Someone with this number operates in a different way from the rest of us. They appear to listen to the beat of a different, somewhat mystical, drum and follow a different path. They are strongly psychic, experiencing powerful intuitions, vivid dreams and an ability to tune into whatever is going on around them. Perhaps for this reason music can play a vital role in their lives, whether they are performers or listeners. Relationships usually go well, provided the partner respects this person's need for solitude and their powerful desire to express themselves creatively. Sevens live inside their heads and their contemplative nature may make them merely absent-minded or distinctly other-worldly.

HEART NUMBER

Life can be difficult for these people because they are frequently misunderstood. No matter how they appear on the surface, they are driven by a strong belief that they're part of something much

larger than themselves. This may make them seem remote or even downright peculiar, but such considerations don't bother them. Music, literature, the arts and the occult mean much more to them than being sociable and may also eventually take precedence over relationships, which can suffer in such a single-minded atmosphere.

EXPRESSION NUMBER

It may take a while to get to know someone with this number, because at first they will seem rather reflective, distant and reserved. Fear of being rebuffed can deter you from getting any closer to them, yet once you succeed in breaking the ice, you will discover someone who is warm, friendly and fascinating. They are interested in the occult and may display an uncanny ability for piercing the surface of things to tap their essence.

EIGHT

An extremely powerful number, Eight is linked with the material world, destiny and infinity. It is associated with the planet Saturn, the sign of Capricorn and dark colours such as charcoal grey and black.

DESTINY NUMBER

Status is very important for these people. Even if they have a relatively unimportant job, they must know that it will eventually lead to something better. They aren't afraid of hard work and often succeed through sheer grit. Eights are the great achievers in life, the people who doggedly follow their dreams until they finally turn them into reality. This may be at the expense of satisfactory relationships, which have to take a back seat to the person's ambitions. The result is often a Pyrrhic victory – the Eight achieves plenty of material success but has no one to share it with.

PERSONALITY NUMBER

This person needs to be in control of their surroundings, and usually is. They have excellent organizational skills, being able to motivate not only themselves to extraordinary lengths but also everyone around them. Their streak of perfectionism can get them far, although they may reach their goal alone – partners and associates will have fallen by the wayside long before, either unable to match the relentless pace or isolated by

their over-riding need for material success. So, Eights must learn to relax more in relationships.

HEART NUMBER

It is important for this person to believe that they are a success in whatever they choose to do, otherwise their strong inner drive and ambition will be thwarted, leading to bitterness and deep dissatisfaction. They need the material benefits of life and may feel cheated when they have to make do with second best. At home, this person is the boss, organizing the running of the household and ensuring that everyone obeys their orders. In relationships, they are loyal and dependable but may be rather imperious, especially if they think their partner isn't pulling their weight.

EXPRESSION NUMBER

Here is someone with a powerful need for worldly achievement, who usually succeeds, especially in big business. They are highly respected in their career because they are not afraid of hard work and have excellent organizational abilities. They value money, and the things it can buy, very highly and devote a great deal of energy to keeping the bank account as healthy as possible. Forget about keeping up with the Joneses – these people *are* the Joneses. But unfortunately, this can make them appear snobby and superior, winning them few friends.

NINE

Nine is the number of the universe and of vision. It represents spiritual ideals, philosophy and perfection. It is linked with the planet Mars, and therefore with the signs of Aries and Scorpio. Its colours are all shades of red.

DESTINY NUMBER
These people are inspired visionaries, full of energy and enterprise, and have the enthusiasm needed to keep working on their ambitions until they reach fruition. They are achievers, although they may find it easier to come up with the ideas than to follow them through to completion – usually, someone else ends up carrying out Nines' brilliant schemes. Nines are competitive and enjoy rising to a challenge, which they generally win. They have often had difficult childhoods and experience life as a series of distinct cycles of good and bad times. After a bad cycle, the Nine will feel despondent for a while before embarking, with fresh hope, on the next major cycle. They may have several careers in the course of their life. Nines can lack consideration for others, which may cause problems in relationships.

PERSONALITY NUMBER
These people have strong humanitarian and philanthropic ideals, and a deep need to work for the common good, which may take many unusual forms. Nines are also practical, thanks to their talent for organization and the ability to make things happen. They enjoy travelling and may spend months exploring a country and getting to know its people. Nines have powerful visionary tendencies but can sometimes be impatient for the desired results, which makes them chivvy others along. This does not always go down well, and can reflect badly on them. They usually have a few deep secrets that they don't want anyone else to know, and enjoy cloak-and-dagger encounters.

HEART NUMBER
These people have an insatiable curiosity, especially about how things work. They are always analysing everyone's motives and watching to see what will happen next, and why. This can harm their relationships, as partners may feel like specimens under a microscope. Nevertheless, Nines are extremely romantic and loving. They also have an inner need to help others and will feel frustrated if this urge can't be expressed.

EXPRESSION NUMBER
It's hard to ignore these people because they are so lively, vivacious and charming. They also have a strong regard for the truth, which can make them forthright to the point of bluntness, yet somehow they are always forgiven. Despite this, they are very understanding and may be selfless on occasion. At other times, they can become completely wrapped up in themselves and insensitive to anyone's needs but their own. Personal freedom is very important to them, and sometimes this may extend to infidelity.

ELEVEN

The first of the two master numbers, Eleven represents spiritual insights, revelations and psychic gifts. It is linked with Uranus, the sign of Aquarius and its colours are sky blue, grey and silver.

DESTINY NUMBER

Because this number is composed of two Ones, these people are amply endowed with all the leadership qualities of Ones, and are resolutely determined to achieve whatever it is they set out to do. What's more, they usually succeed, because they are prepared to take risks and will work around the clock if necessary until they obtain their objective. This single-minded determination earns them a great deal of respect and acclaim from others. Warm and lively, they are popular and may have an enormous influence over the other people in their life – Elevens are special. They should beware of exploiting these attributes for selfish, materialistic or idealistic purposes.

PERSONALITY NUMBER

These people are excellent communicators and are often drawn to the world of the media. This is the number of the idealist, and Elevens may want to spread a particular message, in which case they should ensure that their innate ability to influence others is used in positive and wise ways. Close relationships may be a stumbling block because these people are usually so wrapped up in their ambitions that friendships have to take second place. They may also be rather bossy.

HEART NUMBER

No matter how these people may appear on the surface, they are secretly on an idealistic quest to change the world for the better, in whichever way most appeals. What's more, they won't be deflected from this and will stick to their guns no matter how difficult that might be, or what sacrifices they will have to make along the way. This gives them enormous reserves of inner strength and they're justified in being quite convinced that they will succeed in the end. Such single-mindedness may cause nervous tension.

EXPRESSION NUMBER

These people are idealists who are determined to stick to their principles. This can make them an

inspiration to others, especially if they turn their talents towards something which brings out their rich seam of creativity. This artistic streak can result in great acclaim and success, or it may turn the person into a dreamer who never achieves anything and who lacks direction. They are particularly sensitive to spiritual matters and are able to incorporate this awareness into their everyday lives. This sensitivity can also make them highly strung and nervous. Sometimes they can be rather dogmatic, wanting to impose their ideas on others without considering their feelings.

TWENTY-TWO

The second of the two master numbers, Twenty-two is the number of perfection and also of the builder, both physically and metaphorically. It is linked to the planet Neptune, and to the sign of Pisces. Its colours are purple and mauve.

DESTINY NUMBER

These people are very capable, industrious and practical, and have the ability to realize their full potential. However, the continual battles with the varying energies that are within them, and the constant need to achieve a sense of balance in their life, can conflict with their desire for accomplishment and success, and may eventually mean that they achieve less than they set out to do. They may spend their early years trying to earn some easy money only to realize, when they are much older, that a great deal of their potential remains untapped. They are interesting companions but their tremendous drive can sometimes make them difficult to live with.

PERSONALITY NUMBER

It's hard to ignore these people, partly because of their charisma and magnetism, and partly because they usually make a tremendous success of their lives. They have the ambition and determination to get to the top of whichever area of life they concentrate on, although they should avoid resting on their laurels, giving up halfway through a project or assuming that they know more than they do about a subject. In relationships, they may be slow to commit themselves, which can be frustrating for their partner, who won't know where they stand. Once committed, however, they are extremely faithful.

HEART NUMBER

A tremendous amount of potential simmers away inside these people, but the burning question is whether they will make the most of it or take the easy way out and settle for a series of half-hearted ventures or careers. They certainly have the intelligence to succeed if they try. They also have a strong need to do things that will benefit mankind. In relationships, they can be rather overpowering yet, conversely, they have a deep need for peace and harmony.

EXPRESSION NUMBER

Charming, intelligent and far more capable of standing on their own two feet than they appear, these people are shrewd judges of situations and also of characters. They are extremely popular, and their charisma and air of innocence make them stand out from the crowd. They are idealists who like to work for the common good in some way, even if on a very subtle level. Despite being aware of the spiritual side of life, these people often succeed materially, provided they can surmount their inferiority complexes.

LIVING WITH NUMEROLOGY

There are many ways to use numerology in your life. For instance, not only can you calculate someone's name and birthdate, but you can also calculate how a particular year will affect them. All you have to do is add the day and month of the person's birth to the year in question. Imagine, for example, that someone born on 7 April wants to know what the year 1999 will bring them. Here's what you do:

$$7 + 4 + 1 + 9 + 9 + 9 = 39$$
$$3 + 9 = 12$$
$$1 + 2 = 3$$

So, the number for 1999 is Three, suggesting that this person will have a year of great happiness. Things in general should go well for them and life will be very busy.

You can also use this technique to see what was happening in the past. For instance, if 1985 was a particularly memorable year for you, you can add it to your day and month of birth to see what numerology has to say on the subject.

It's fascinating to calculate the destiny and personality numbers of people you know. Once you start to apply what you've read here to friends and relations, numerology will take on extra significance. You'll read about the characteristics of each number and relate them to people you know and, once you become familiar with numerology, you may develop an instinctive sense of what some people's numbers will be. You might also realize that certain numbers crop up again and again in your circle of friends and family, while others aren't represented by anyone. Is there an obvious reason for this? When you read the descriptions of these missing numbers you may instinctively feel that you aren't attuned to them.

Another interesting exercise is to calculate the numbers for someone who has changed their name. A woman's name often changes when she gets married but the situation can apply to anyone who has altered a significant part of their name or added an initial. If all the numbers of their old and new names match, the change hasn't affected their personality at all. If the names do have different numbers, can you relate them both to the person concerned?

The person who successfully replaces the numerological significance of their old name with their new one has an extremely strong personality. Very often, you will find echoes of the old name in the new one. For instance, the expression number of a woman's maiden name and the personality number of her married name may both be Nine. So this suggests that the marriage has given this woman a great deal of emotional satisfaction because it's enabled her to express her inner desires.

If things aren't going well for you, or you feel there's a conflict between one of the numbers in your name and your true personality, see if some slight adjustments (such as a different spelling or the use of a nickname) will help to create a number that suits you better. To see the effects that this can have on someone's life, try calculating the numbers of famous people who've changed their names – such as John Wayne, who started life as Marion Michael Morrison; Woody Allen, whose parents know him as Allen Stewart Konigsberg; or Michael Caine, who was born Maurice Micklewhite.

As you become more confident and familiar with numerology, you'll realize how useful it can be. It may also help you to see patterns and structures in everything around you, including the most significant events in your life. You could call it living by numbers.

Pendulums

The art of dowsing – the ability to locate objects using a pendulum or

forked twig – is ancient. No one knows when it was first practised,

although the Roman authors Cicero and Tacitus both wrote of the

ability to make predictions using sticks. The earliest surviving

reference to dowsing appeared in fifteenth-century Germany,

when forked twigs were used by prospectors hunting for

minerals. Of all the techniques in this book, dowsing has

perhaps the most conventional backing – in the form of

water companies, many of whom now employ dowsers to

detect leaking pipes and underground springs. Dowsing

with the help of a pendulum is a fascinating

introduction to this art, and enables you to tune into

your intuition, often with remarkable results.

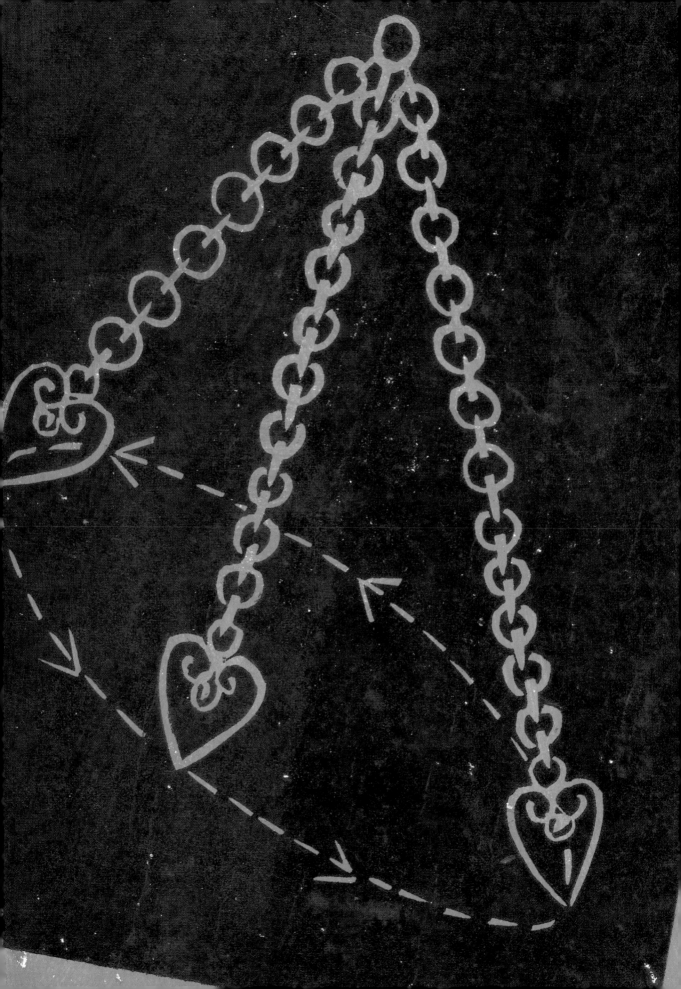

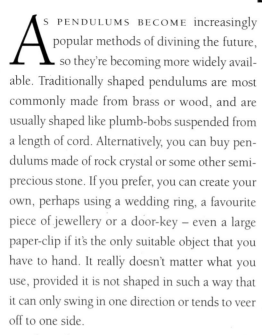

As pendulums become increasingly popular methods of divining the future, so they're becoming more widely available. Traditionally shaped pendulums are most commonly made from brass or wood, and are usually shaped like plumb-bobs suspended from a length of cord. Alternatively, you can buy pendulums made of rock crystal or some other semi-precious stone. If you prefer, you can create your own, perhaps using a wedding ring, a favourite piece of jewellery or a door-key – even a large paper-clip if it's the only suitable object that you have to hand. It really doesn't matter what you use, provided it is not shaped in such a way that it can only swing in one direction or tends to veer off to one side.

When choosing a suitable pendulum, you need one that is heavy enough to be carried along by its own momentum and to swing in a definite arc without being blown off-course by sudden sighs from you or gusts of wind from an open window. You should also choose a pendulum that you like and feel comfortable with – if you aren't happy with your pendulum you won't use it.

If you've bought a classic plumb-bob pendulum, it will already have a piece of cord attached to it. If, however, you are devising your own you must choose a length of ribbon or cord that is long enough and smooth enough to allow the pendulum to swing freely. Experiment with the length of the cord until it feels comfortable to use. In general, the heavier the pendulum, the longer the cord. Avoid anything that has a rough texture, as the pendulum could snag on this and not swing properly.

Opinion is divided about what you should do with your pendulum when it's not in use. Some people leave theirs in a safe place, awaiting their call. Others carry it with them at all times, reasoning that they never know when they'll need it.

They may also believe that always having the pendulum with them impregnates it with their vibrations and therefore makes it more sensitive. However, there are no rules about this, so do whatever seems most natural to you.

HOW TO USE THE PENDULUM

The beauty of the pendulum lies in its ability to only answer 'yes', 'no' or 'maybe' to a question. At first, you may think that this gives it a very limited appeal. What is the point of something that can only respond in such a bald way, you might wonder. However, once you begin to experiment with a pendulum you'll realize that there are times when 'yes' or 'no' is the only answer you want – it is precisely this categorical response that can point you in the right direction. Sometimes you need the subtlety and layers of meaning that you can only get from reading the tarot or playing cards. At other times these forms of divination may not be immediate enough for your needs. For instance, if you can't decide whether to accept the new job that's been offered to you, the pendulum will give you a straight, no-nonsense answer. After that, you can use a more complex technique if you want to investigate your options further.

When you want to use a pendulum, the first thing you should do is to discover how it's going to respond to your questions. In order to do this, you must ask it to demonstrate its various responses. These are the search position, 'yes', 'no' and 'maybe'. You can do this either out loud or mentally, if someone happens to be within earshot and you don't want to attract any funny looks.

Hold the top of the cord or ribbon between your thumb and forefinger, letting the pendulum hang down – you may find it easiest if you rest

Illustration from Georgius Agricola's De Re Metallica, *showing sixteenth-century dowsers searching for metallic ores*

Examples of how the pendulum may swing. Top left: 'No' response (left to right swing). Top right: 'Yes' response (backwards and forwards swing). Bottom right: 'Maybe' response (elliptical swing).

your elbow on a table. Make sure the pendulum is still, then ask it to show you its search position. It will either stay still or start to move. Make a note of this.

Now ask the pendulum to show you its 'yes' response. If you wish, you can do this by asking the pendulum a precise question to which you know the answer can only be in the affirmative. (For instance, you could ask it if a wooden table is made from wood.) The pendulum will start to move – if it doesn't, swing it in a circular direction and then watch to see what movement it settles into. It might swing backwards and forwards, or from side to side. Do this a couple of times to check that this is definitely the 'yes' response.

Repeat the process to discover the 'no' response. Once again, ask a question to which the only answer can be in the negative – you could now ask the pendulum if the table you're sitting at is made of cream cheese. The pendulum will start to swing in a direction that's different from the 'yes' response. For instance, if 'yes' is a swing backwards and forwards, 'no' could be a swing from left to right. Check this a couple of times, to ensure that both you and the pendulum are clear about what means 'no'.

Now ask the pendulum to show you its fourth response, which you can interpret as 'maybe' or 'stupid question'. It is simple to do this – ask it a silly question. If the pendulum doesn't move, start to swing it in a circular direction, then watch its movement. It might be elliptical, or it could be diagonal. You now have the four pendulum responses, and you should keep practising them every day for about a week, so you're completely familiar with them.

Sometimes, the pendulum can play a little game with you, muddling up its responses or playing possum. If this happens, you need to be firm with it and ask it to co-operate. This may sound bizarre yet what you're really doing is instructing your subconscious, not the pendulum, to try harder. If, after this, the pendulum continues to give you a nonsensical response, you may decide that it's not a good time to ask your question and that you should try again later.

No matter how many times you've used a pendulum, you should always check how it's going to respond before you ask it any questions. Sometimes it will change the direction of its 'yes', 'no' and 'maybe' swings, and this can cause havoc if you aren't aware of what is going on.

Keep practising with the pendulum, so you can get used to each other. When you're confident that you know the direction of each response, you can hold the pendulum and ask it to move from 'yes' to 'no' to 'maybe/wrong question', back to 'yes', and so on, and it will obediently follow your instructions. At this stage, you are consciously influencing the swing of the pendulum, but that doesn't matter because you aren't dowsing for anything, you are simply mastering how to use the pendulum.

ASKING THE RIGHT QUESTIONS

One of the most common problems for people getting accustomed to using a pendulum is that they ask it the wrong question. Always remember that it can only answer 'yes', 'no' or 'maybe/wrong question', so there's no point in asking something like, 'Should I buy the pink scarf or the black suit?' It will either refuse to co-operate at all or give you the 'wrong question' response.

You should also be as specific as possible when asking a question. If you looked at three black suits in the course of your shopping trip then you should specify which one it is you're thinking of buying. Otherwise, the pendulum may again become confused. Remember that the answer can only ever be as good as the question.

HOW THE PENDULUM WORKS

By now, you may be thinking that the pendulum has obviously become anthropomorphized by the people who use it. Otherwise, how on earth could it get confused by the wrong question?

To appreciate this, you have to understand how the pendulum works. Or, rather, how it may work – no one knows for certain. When it's sitting on a table or in a box, a pendulum is simply an inanimate object. And that condition doesn't change when you hold its cord between your fingers. However, when you ask it a question, something takes over. Everyone has a theory as to what this is, but as yet there are no conclusive answers.

One popular theory is that the pendulum acts as a link to your subconscious, enabling you to tune into ideas and knowledge that your conscious mind is unaware of or has screened out. When you ask your question, your subconscious responds by sending minute electrical impulses down your arm, and these influence the swing of the pendulum. You will already have experienced this if you've been making the pendulum change the direction of its swing. You will also experience it if you ask the pendulum a question in which you have a vested emotional interest – unless you can distract yourself, the answer will always be the one you want to hear.

Other theories are that some form of radar is working (this seems quite possible if you're using the pendulum to dowse for water or a lost object); that you've tuned into the Akashic Records (the term first given by Rudolf Steiner to the esoteric concept of a cosmic 'library' that contains records of absolutely everything that's ever happened in the world); or that your guardian angel, or maybe your long-dead Aunt Dorothy, is giving you the answers.

Whether any or none of these theories is correct doesn't alter the fact that the pendulum does actually work. However, if you tell yourself that it is unscientific and therefore can't work, you have just ensured that it won't. So, don't worry about how or why it works, simply concentrate on the fact that it does.

PRACTICE MAKES PERFECT

Like all the other predictive techniques described in this book, it takes practice to use the pendulum. Sadly, when you start you may get more wrong answers than right ones – you need to train yourself to use it properly. That's especially true if you plan to use the pendulum as a predictive tool for other people. Although when using other techniques in this book, such as cartomancy, you can refer to the text if you get stuck or forget what something means, you can't do that in the same way with the pendulum. The link between it and your subconscious instincts and intuitions is too direct for that, so you must strengthen this link before you can use it to give guidance to other people. Otherwise, you may mistakenly give them the wrong information.

If you don't have fun using your pendulum, it will stay in its box or will merely gather dust on a tabletop. So start practising with it, using any question that relies on 'yes' and 'no' answers. As well as asking your pendulum obvious questions to which there's only one rational answer ('Is my left hand touching the fridge?', 'Am I standing on my head?', 'Is it Wednesday today?'), you can also consult it on more complex issues. One good test is to take a deck of ordinary playing cards and shuffle them, then hold the pendulum over the back of each one in turn and ask it if the card is red. Sort the cards into piles accordingly, then check the results. At first, you will probably make a complete hash of this, but keep practising. After a few tries, you'll find that your results are improving significantly, especially if you treat the

Frontispiece from Johann Zeidler's
Pantomysterium *(meaning 'The Universal
Mystery Teaching') of 1700, showing the author,
who was himself a dowser*

exercise more as an enjoyable game than an exam. For some reason, the harder you try with a pendulum, the less likely it is to co-operate.

A good exercise at this stage is to use the pendulum to sort objects. Take three identical envelopes and draw a big cross on the back of one, then shuffle them and place them face up on a table. Use your pendulum to find which carries the cross. Try the same thing with three identical boxes containing dice.

You can do this in one of two ways. The laborious process is to hold the pendulum over the first item, putting it in the search position and then seeing what response it gives you, before repeating the procedure with the second item, and so on. The quicker process, which is useful when you want to dowse a large area, is to hold the pendulum above all the items and see which way it swings. To do this, arrange the items roughly in a circle, hold the pendulum above them in the search position and watch its swing. It will probably start off with a wide ellipse (which means 'I'm getting close') and go into a circle (meaning 'Found it!') when you hold it above the object you are dowsing for, before returning to an ellipse when you move it away.

Dowsing in this way takes practice, so try to do at least one exercise every day until you're proficient. You can ask a willing helper to hide a specific object in a room, and then you can dowse for it by moving around the room and watching the swing of the pendulum turn from the search position into an ellipse to a circle (as shown on page 186), or whichever movements your pendulum adopts to show you its responses. You could also use the pendulum to see if there's any money in your wallet.

Keep practising until your results start to beat the statistics and your answers are more often right than wrong. Don't assume you will always be right – it's unlikely. The pendulum isn't a magic wand or an infallible way of getting at the truth; it is a means of tuning into your subconscious to discover answers that you didn't know you knew. And sometimes, for any number of reasons, those answers may turn out to be wrong.

DOWSING WITH THE PENDULUM

Once you become comfortable with it, the pendulum can help you in all sorts of ways. You can use it when choosing tarot cards, for instance;

USING THE PENDULUM TO SEARCH FOR AND LOCATE OBJECTS

1 Search position	**3** Circle	**5** Ellipse
2 Ellipse	**4** Target	**6** Search position

shuffle the cards and lay them face down in front of you, then use your pendulum to choose which cards you should read. Put it in the search position over the first card, then ask 'Is this card significant for me today?' Move the pendulum, still swinging, over each card and choose the ones to which you get a 'yes' response. Make a note of the cards you've selected and how apt they are.

People who work with aromatherapy oils and Bach flower remedies often use pendulums to choose which oils to give their patients. You could do the same for yourself, although you should always check its suitability before using it.

If you're undecided about which piece of music to listen to, or which video to watch, you can ask your pendulum to choose. Place one hand on the video or CD and hold the pendulum with the other. If you get a 'yes' response, are you happy with that?

SEARCHING

A pendulum is a particularly valuable tool when searching for lost objects. Instead of turning the house upside down looking for your contact lens case (particularly inconvenient if your lenses happen to be in it at the time), ask your pendulum to do the hard work for you. You can either take your pendulum into each room in turn or simply stay in one place and ask about each room in turn, mentally picturing each room as you ask about it. Once you've narrowed down the search, work your way through it systematically, watching the pendulum to see when it changes from the search position to an ellipse, and then finally into a circle.

If you've ever waited impatiently for a friend to arrive, you will know how irritating this can be. With a pendulum, however, this becomes much easier, because you can hold it in the search position and call out the hours – once it says 'yes' to

a particular hour, you can then dowse to find the quarter-hour or even the exact minute.

You can dowse a map to find someone's location, too. For instance, if you know that they're somewhere on the road between their house and yours, you can dowse that area on a map. Hold the pendulum in the search position, then move it gently over the area you are searching and watch its movements change. Experienced dowsers use this method to search for water, minerals, ley lines and many other things besides.

FINDING ANSWERS

Your pendulum can also be used to answer questions about your future, or anyone else's for that matter. However, remember that you will have to detach yourself emotionally from the question in order to receive an objective answer. To do this, fill your mind with something neutral while waiting for your pendulum to respond. Sig Lonegren, the American dowser, suggests repeating to yourself over and over again, 'I wonder what the answer's going to be?' – this will act like mental white noise. Don't think about anything that could evoke an emotional response, such as your forthcoming holiday or what's for supper, because the pendulum might react to that thought.

Most people find that they are more successful with some dowsing techniques than others, so don't give up if you can't dowse hidden objects, for example – you might be gifted at dowsing the answers to questions instead. Learn to enjoy using your pendulum and see which directions it leads you in, but, above all, remember that it is simply a tool that amplifies your intuitions and turns them into a visual message. You can find the answers without the pendulum, if you trust your intuition enough. Perhaps, by the time you have used all the techniques in this book, that is exactly what you will be able to do.

INDEX

Page numbers in *italic* refer to captions

ACKNOWLEDGEMENTS

Writing this book has been a double pleasure. Firstly, because it has allowed me to fulfil an ambition that I've nursed since I was fourteen and should have been concentrating on my education instead of what the stars foretold. Secondly, because it's been such a pleasure to work with everyone on this book. So the following people should line up and take a bow while I give them a well-deserved standing ovation:

A huge bouquet to Cindy Richards who acted as an inspired producer of the whole project. She supplied faith in me, encouragement, glasses of wine and much laughter. Hearty cheers for Alison Wormleighton who sat patiently in the prompt corner, skilfully editing my copy and gently hauling me back on the straight and narrow whenever I fluffed my lines. Thunderous applause for my old friend Roger Daniels who designed the whole production. I'd like to say what a terrific designer he is but I don't want to embarrass him. An extra curtain call for the highly talented Jacqui Mair, for her luscious illustrations. Take a bow, Muna Reyal, who was a sunny-tempered and ingenious picture-researcher, and I'd also like to applaud everyone else at Collins and Brown who worked on the book. Two other people deserve prolonged applause – my friend and agent Chelsey Fox, who suggested the book to me in the first place and should have a huge star pinned to her office door; and my husband, Bill Martin, who was the best kind of stage-door Johnny. Finally, drum rolls for Tom Petty and the Rolling Stones, to celebrate their musical accompaniments while I was writing the book.

The publishers would like to thank:
Yasha Beresiner, Intercol London (Gallery), 114 Islington High Street, London N1 for his help with the cartomancy cards.

ILLUSTRATION ACKNOWLEDGEMENTS

All illustrations have been painted specially for this book by Jacqueline Mair, except for the following which appear by kind permission:

Apple Corporation 163

The Bridgeman Art Library: Antonio Cicognara/K & B News Foto, Florence 12

C M Dixon 49

E. T. Archive: Civic Museum Vicenza 130, Glasgow University Library 6, Palazzo Farnese Caprarola 7

Foto Dani, Milan 129

Images Colour Library/The Charles Walker Collection 23, 50, 128, 130, 131, 136, 139, 140, 154, 162, 165, 181, 185 and the border details on pages 128-159 & 162-177

Mary Evans Picture Library 10, 33, 48, 52, 53, 60, 66-67, 158